"PERSONAL" PROPERTY OF
EDWARD G. VERLANDER

More than
Management Development

More than Management Development

Action Learning at GEC

AMACOM

A Division of American Management Associations

© 1977 Teakfield Limited

All rights reserved. No part of this publication may be reproduced, stored in a retrieval system, or transmitted in any form or by any means, electronic, mechanical, photocopying, recording, or otherwise without the prior permission of Teakfield Limited, Westmead, Farnborough, Hampshire, England.

ISBN 0 8144 5446 1

Library of Congress Catalog Card Number 77-70350

Printed in Great Britain by Biddles Ltd, Guildford, Surrey

Contents

Foreword, *Sir Arnold Weinstock* vii
Preface ix

PART ONE   THE ACTION LEARNING PROGRAMME

1 ACTION LEARNING, *Professor Reg Revans*
   The business of learning about business   3
2 PROGRAMME OUTLINE, *David Casey*
   General description of the programme   7
3 PROGRAMME DEVELOPMENT, *David Pearce*
   How the action learning programme was developed at GEC   14

PART TWO   PARTICIPANTS' EXPERIENCES

4 THE PROJECT IS EVERYTHING, *Bill Prince*
   A micro-electronics product policy problem tackled by a manager from another part of GEC   31
5 LEARNING HOW TO LEARN, *Peter Preston*
   Participants from the Post Office and GEC work together   40
6 THIS IS THE WAY TO UNLOCK RESOURCES, *Don Howell*
   A GEC manager is assigned to a major problem in a government department   45

7   IT DIDN'T WORK FOR ME, *David Carr*
    A manager tries to take on his own job as an action
    learning project   48
8   NOW ... TO RUN A COMPANY, *Colin Gaskell*
    A project within his own company, but outside his own job,
    by a GEC manager   58
9   COMMUNICATION IS THE KEY TO GETTING
    COMMITMENT, *Barry Scott*
    A technical manager takes on a systems problem in
    another part of GEC   62

PART THREE   ALP INTERNATIONAL AND DUNCHURCH INDUSTRIAL STAFF COLLEGE

10 THE CHALLENGE WAS WORTH IT, *Ray Godsall*
    What the industrial staff college which housed the
    programme felt   73
11 DON'T CALL ME TEACHER, *Bob Garratt*
    An ALP project adviser's view from his set   79
12 ALP IS LEARNING TOO, *Jean Lawrence*
    A director of ALP International reviews her
    programme involvement   91

PART FOUR   THE IMPACT OF ACTION LEARNING ON GEC

13 WE'D DO IT AGAIN, *Clem Jansen and Don Sinclair*
    Two GEC managers review the project carried out in
    their company   105
14 YOU DON'T NEED TO BE AN EXPERT, *Glyn Trollop*
    GEC's group personnel manager reviews his experiences
    as a set adviser   109
15 IT'S OPENING OUR MINDS, *Mike Bett*
    What the process of action learning has started in GEC   116
16 ACTION LEARNING AND THE COMPANY,
    Professor Tony Eccles
    A project adviser, who is also a professor of business policy,
    takes the broad view   119
POSTSCRIPT: GEC'S SECOND AND THIRD
PROGRAMMES   124

APPENDICES

Appendix I	The offer document	131
Appendix II	Debate between set advisers and GEC staff	135
Appendix III	List of participants and their projects	139
GLOSSARY		145

Foreword

SIR ARNOLD WEINSTOCK, Managing Director, General Electric Company Ltd

Risk-taking leaders with flair are hard to find and difficult to cultivate. Creating the conditions in which they can emerge and flourish has never been more important. As managing director of GEC it is my prime responsibility to ensure that the company has a team of firstclass senior managers who can achieve good results now and in the future.

Experience and observation have convinced me that we learn most when faced with a real problem which we are obliged to solve. These are the circumstances in which we give of our best and in which we are prepared to listen more acutely to the people around us.

In the autumn of 1973, I watched Professor Revans on television illustrating the theories and practice of action learning. He and I met subsequently and embarked on an action learning programme for some managers in GEC. This book is an account of that first experience when 21 managers came together for eight months to tackle difficult projects in our businesses for the purpose of learning rapidly and effectively some of the skills required for senior management.

The real worth of that project and subsequent programmes will not be fully apparent for several years; and any truly valuable experience which leads an individual to modify his approach to managing, or to life in general, may be untidy, indistinct and even painful. The contributions in this book should be read in that light. It would be easy to present a facile series of neatly argued and logically reasoned accounts of what happened; but real life is not like that.

Britain is facing increasing competition from countries where industrial productivity is superior to our own. Our customers at home and overseas expect us to provide the goods they want on time, well finished and at a price which offers good value. To be able to compete successfully we must continuously improve our performance, and that means doing many things differently, even if, as individuals and groups, we often find change uncomfortable.

We will have to learn to create the conditions in which people at all levels can become more meaningfully involved in their work and in an industrial society. We at GEC, and others, are searching for constructive and creative methods of consultation to enable and encourage our people to contribute towards the decisions which materially affect their lives. This is an enlightened development in human relations, but it has to lead to good results at work.

In an age of increasingly complex and expensive technology, people who can pose the right questions and energetically pursue constructive solutions are indispensable in industry. I trust that this book will give encouragement and assistance to those who share our objectives and aspirations. In the last resort, it is only by doing things that we learn what can be done.

Preface

Even before the first GEC action learning programme was halfway through we were amazed by the level of interest shown. An open-house attitude was kept throughout; over 50 visitors, many from overseas, wanted to know what we were doing and how people were reacting. A far greater number of people have heard about the programme but were not able to come and see us at work. This book is the response to some of the questions we know to be in their minds. It was written by people who spent a year or so in the experiment, and it records their experiences and feelings.

In editing this book we decided not to stick too rigidly to a preconceived structure, preferring instead to suggest a few basic themes which the writers could use in expressing their very personal viewpoints. One such theme was the growth and development of individuals. In any action learning programme the individual is faced with two learning situations. He learns in the awful loneliness of his project (where he spends most of his time) and in a quite different way in the small 'set' (to which he retreats once every week to spend a full day in close comradeship with his fellow adventurers). Some writers were asked to say what they had learned from their project work; others were asked to focus on their 'set' meetings.

Another main theme is the impact which action learning had on the businesses which offered themselves up for investigation and change. This, again, is a process of learning. Just as a person learns by taking action and reflecting on the consequences, so a business learns by doing things differently and considering the results. But while an individual can be asked to write down his experiences, a more difficult task is to capture on paper the learning processes of organizations. We knew that we had to overcome this problem; the resulting chapters should prove helpful to others setting out on action learning programmes of their own.

Our programme was a venture into management development for over 20 managers, and an organizational development exercise for GEC. The projects carried out in GEC are still live issues, central to the success of many GEC businesses. We could have waited for five years for all the facts and figures to emerge. But this would have been picking over the dry bones of dead issues; we preferred instead to write quickly about what we are all feeling now.

We emphasize the learning side of action learning because this is what people ask us about. But the action side is likely to become even more important in the long run. In the future it could be an outcome more clearly identified and more intuitively sought after by top managers. Perhaps the business action in action learning is the missing touchstone of management development which has eluded us in Britain for so long. We all know how crucial is the support from top management. It could be that action in their businesses — on their most pressing problems — is the only way that management development will ever penetrate to the hearts and guts of top managers (as distinct from their heads). Action learning provides that way in.

Part One introduces the concept of action learning and describes the programme. Part Two is the core of the book, written by a selection of programme participants, chosen to present a representative cross-section of reactions (ranging, in fact, from near cynicism to blatant euphoria). Part Three is devoted to the experiences of two outside organizations, ALP International and Dunchurch Industrial Staff College. Finally, in Part Four, the programme is examined from within GEC.

David Casey
David Pearce

Part One
The action learning programme

1
Action learning

The business of learning about business

PROFESSOR REG REVANS

> Action learning is well known but little understood. One major application is described in this book. There are, of course, others. All are very different in character, but all share one common ingredient — Professor Reg Revans.
> R. W. Revans, MIMinE, DSc, formerly Fellow of Emmanuel College, Cambridge, and Professor of Industrial Administration at the University of Manchester, is now Visiting Professor of Praxiology, University of Leeds.

Major programmes in action learning — whereby those responsible for getting things done learn with and from each other while getting them done — have now been started in Belgium, Egypt, India, Libya, Saudi Arabia, the United States and Great Britain, where GEC have mounted the exercise that this book is about, so setting an example that others have decided to follow.

Action learning

Action learning differs from traditional courses of management education in several ways:

1 It is concerned with taking specific action as well as with *talking about* taking some general class of action.
2 Because specific action must be taken by specific persons, those engaged in action learning gain insight not only into their problems

but also into their individual perceptions of and personal responses to such problems.
3 In action learning the majority of time is given both to diagnosing in the field what the problem may be (so challenging the value systems of those caught up in it) and to applying any solutions to the problem that may be suggested (so challenging the validity of such proposals). In traditional programmes held away from the field, diagnosis is generally assumed and application necessarily ignored.
4 Action learning is vitally concerned with the posing of effective questions in working conditions of ignorance, confusion and uncertainty. It is interested in what cannot be seen in the problem no less than in any existing evidence. The necessary processes of field search and of operational test demand the practical confrontation of those responsible for treating the problem; since traditional programmes must avoid both field search and operational test, they compensate with a sophisticated solution to the supposed diagnosis. This often gives to the classroom discussion a ring of incisive sufficiency not wholly compatible with the real situation.

As might be expected, the designs of the various programmes have differed widely among themselves. But all have two common elements: first, participating managers work on problems to which nobody knows any final answer but to which several series of acceptable next moves may be suggested; second, these managers meet each other regularly and on equal terms to report to and to argue with each other about their problems and their progress. At every moment of their involvement they remain firmly in contact with reality, not only as observers of it but as those responsible for changing it in some preferred direction. Whatever theoretical innovations are brought to the participants, by the academic or consulting staff who organize their programmes, are therefore linked to the unsympathetic imperatives of action. And nobody need be afraid that this implies a constriction of vision or an illiberality of value; responsible engagement with reality is a powerful multiplier of intellectual dimensions.

Aims of action learning

So much for a comparison of action learning with the traditions of education and for an outline of its logistical approach. But what, essentially, is action learning trying to do? And to what extent is it doing it? These are fundamental questions, the kind from which most systems of higher education modestly avert their gaze. We set out, in action learning, to achieve three distinct goals:

1 To help experienced managers, as individuals, perceive more clearly and control more effectively their responses to situations in which, at the outset, nobody knows what to do.
2 To help the management staff of an enterprise or other organization use more effectively its existing resources, in cooperation with a participant manager not normally employed by that enterprise.
3 To help the training staffs of the participating enterprises, as well as the faculty of any school or other academic institution involved in the programme, to see in a new light their roles in developing effective managers.

These are no doubt limited goals; first, to encourage managers to find their bearings quickly in situations of confusion and obscurity, where there is neither initial agreement about nor understanding of what to do for the best. Second, to help a management perceive more realistically its own strengths and weaknesses, its own internal dynamics and resistances, so that from its present assets it may make useful progress with problems so far proved insoluble. Third, to reveal the training staff of an enterprise as those who enable management to learn from everyday experience. But one advantage of a limited list of aspirations is that it may be tested more readily than an expansive one. So modest a set of claims should, therefore, soon be the subject of rigorous and disinterested proof, probably by one of the monitoring agencies now officially set up (rather late in the day, perhaps) in Britain to check whether any effects, good or bad, have flowed from our previous expenditures on management education.

For the present, however, our verifications of action learning must remain subjective, even if the criteria for judging their success remain the three here set out. Yet in all countries a majority of individual managers who followed the programmes have shown some enlargement of vision; a few among them have revealed quite unsuspected and even spectacular talents in the course of tackling their unseen problems. Opinion is divided upon whether or not the unseen problems are brought more effectively under control by having been worked on as action learning projects. The one statistically verifiable exercise in the field — an action learning project among hospitals — shows that participating institutions improved their performance very significantly more than did a control group of similar hospitals that did not participate. And it appears that, if one is prepared to wait a year or more to let the effect of the action learning project soak well into the enterprise, informed opinion normally moves towards supporting its long-term outcome. Finally, the industrial training staffs, without exception, and a majority of the cooperating academic faculty, are agreed that their parts in the problem-attacking projects have given them an insight into their own professional roles that they could not have secured in any way — other than by becoming involved with experienced managers as they seek the understanding and support of colleagues equally in need. And a further mark of worthwhileness may be that, at a time when most other forms of management development are encountering severe discouragement (and not a few the ferocious denunciation of erstwhile backers) action learning is extending itself across the world. Norway, Sweden, Malaysia, South Africa and Australia are now starting to experiment: they, too, have come round to the opinion of St James (Epistle 1:22):

> But be ye doers of the word and not hearers only, deceiving your own selves. For if any be a hearer of the word, and not a doer, he is like unto a man beholding his natural face in a glass. For he beholdeth himself and goeth his way, and straightway forgetteth what manner of man he was.

Let us hope that an impartial evaluation of our efforts with GEC may soon verify this immemorial statement of an obvious but forgettable truth.

2
Programme outline

General description of the programme

DAVID CASEY

> Action learning at GEC occupied many senior people from a large number of different organizations in a programme that was complex, used new learning philosophies, and must be described with a new set of technical terms. David Casey was programme coordinator for ALP. In this chapter he gives an outline of the programme and the roles played by all those concerned with its execution.
>
> David Casey is a director of Action Learning Projects International. His fields are management development and organization development and he has worked inside large companies such as Reed International. He now works freelance and is on the executive of the Association of Teachers of Management.

Translating the concept of action learning into a programme of action is exciting and challenging work. It is also highly complex. This chapter gives a simple outline description, so that the big picture can be appreciated quickly before the more detailed account in the next chapter.

Origins

Sir Arnold Weinstock saw Professor Revans on television, and the two men met very soon afterwards. Sir Arnold was convinced that action learning was right for GEC, but Revans advised Sir Arnold not to coerce GEC into action learning. 'Let the idea stand on its own merits', he suggested.

David Pearce had been recently appointed in GEC as management

GEC...

Found participants and projects and connected the two. Found GEC project advisers. Designed and operated the programme. Helped participants' re-entry.

ALP...

Supported GEC in designing and operating the programme. Responsible for both residential courses and for providing external project advisers. Helped GEC to learn. Did not wish to help a second time.

DISC...

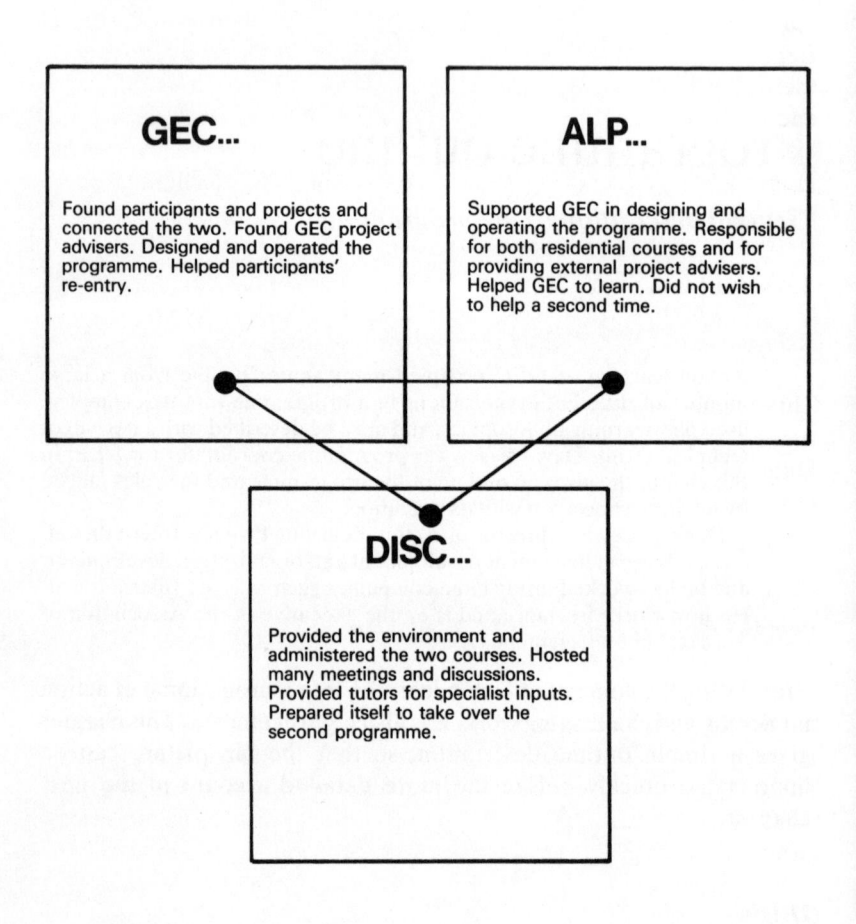

Provided the environment and administered the two courses. Hosted many meetings and discussions. Provided tutors for specialist inputs. Prepared itself to take over the second programme.

Figure 2 : 1 Organizations involved

development adviser and he and I were next involved in mapping out a programme concept, to be agreed by Mike Bett, personnel director, and Sir Arnold. This happened quickly. The concept was taken by Bett and Revans on a tour of senior managing directors who responded in different ways but with enough excitement to convince Bett that Sir Arnold was right — GEC was open to action learning.

Finally, a group of personnel directors from GEC companies visited Belgium with David Pearce to talk directly with those involved over there. They too were convinced. David Pearce now felt he knew enough to put together a tentative prospectus for the first GEC action learning programme. He called this an 'offer document' (see Appendix I) and the response to its circulation in GEC was excellent. Action learning was under way.

Relationships between the organizations involved

Three main organizations cooperated to make the programme a success — GEC, Action Learning Projects International (ALP) and Dunchurch Industrial Staff College (DISC). The roles which these organizations played are shown in Figure 2 : 1.

People involved

Literally hundreds of people were involved. 21 participants, working full time for eight months, engaged the active involvement of at least 10 members of their client organizations; over 200 people for a start. Those principally concerned with organizing the programme from GEC, ALP and DISC are mentioned here by name. Participants, grouped in their sets, are listed in Appendix III.

GEC head office

Sir Arnold Weinstock	Managing director
Michael Bett	Personnel director
Glyn Trollope	Group personnel manager (GEC project adviser)
David Pearce	Management development adviser (Coordinator)

Personnel directors of GEC operating companies

Nigel Eldred	GEC project adviser
James Pease-Watkin	GEC project adviser
John Shrigley	GEC project adviser
Len Grice	Initial preparatory work

Directors of ALP

Professor Reg Revans	Adviser to the whole programme
David Casey	Coordinator and ALP project adviser
Jean Lawrence	ALP project adviser

ALP resources

Professor Tony Eccles	ALP project adviser
Bob Garratt	ALP project adviser

DISC

Ray Godsall	Director
John Teire	Coordinator

A list such as this does little to explain the process by which the programme was managed. Indeed there are not enough sides to a piece of paper to explain the dynamics of such a process — even if we fully understood it ourselves. As with any other large-scale project, success depended entirely on relationships and cooperative efforts. If credit for the grand idea had to be lodged somewhere it must surely go to Reg Revans. If the motivation for GEC's grand decision had to be allocated somewhere, it would lie with Sir Arnold Weinstock, and he passed the responsibility to Mike Bett. For the rest there was a managing group (although we never called it such), which attracted to its councils at different times different people pertinent to the decisions which had to be made next. In a sense the programme seemed bigger than any of our parochial interests, and once launched it generated its own momentum, to which everyone made his or her best contribution.

Basic shape of the programme

The idea was that participants should devote themselves full time for about three months to the diagnosis of a complex and important business problem on their own. But one day each week they would share fully all that was happening to them, in a group called a set composed of four or five others similarly engaged. Two project advisers would be there to help, one from ALP and one from GEC. After diagnosis, an equal period of time would be devoted to implementing the preferred solution. Again, the participant was nominally alone, but by this time he had marshalled the powerful help of members from his client organization, and he was acting as a catalyst to their own self-help.

Twenty-one participants were the nominal 'students' on this programme, organized in four sets geographically. When the sets came together we referred to the 'learning community' as the sum of the participants plus those organizing the programme. But of course there were many other learners, particularly in the client companies, where the projects were carried out. Without question the most powerful learning arenas were the client companies and the project sets. This is represented in Figure 2 : 2. The fulltime work was done here, with four days each week spent in the client company and the remaining day in the project set.

All four sets were occasionally brought together at DISC. Two residential courses were held there. The first of these was to open the programme, and the second at mid-point. Also we invented the idea of two-day workshops, organized entirely by the participants. These also took place at DISC. An outline idea of the base learning community, as it mustered at Dunchurch, is shown in Figure 2 : 3.

Timescale

A full timetable is given in the offer document (see Appendix I). The key dates were as follows:

November 1973	First meeting between Professor Revans and Sir Arnold Weinstock.
May 1974	Participants and projects named.
October 1974	Opening residential course at DISC.
November 1974 to January 1975	Diagnosis of projects. Sets met regularly.
February 1975	Mid-programme residential course at DISC.
March 1975 to May 1975	Implementation of projects. Regular set meetings resumed.

12   *PROGRAMME OUTLINE*

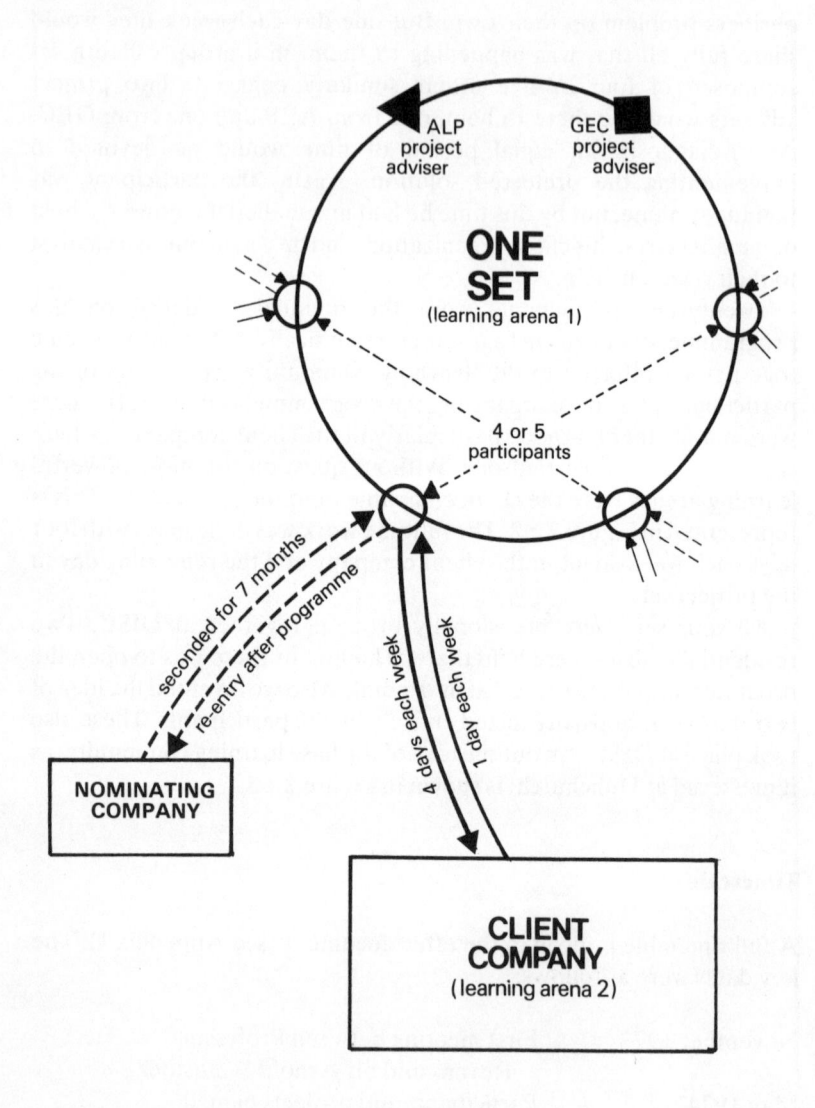

Figure 2 : 2 Two learning arenas

For each project participant there were two places of learning. One day a week was spent in the set and the other four days were spent in the client company, on the project. Some participants took up another option from that depicted here and remained in their own companies (the options available are shown in Appendix I).

PROGRAMME OUTLINE

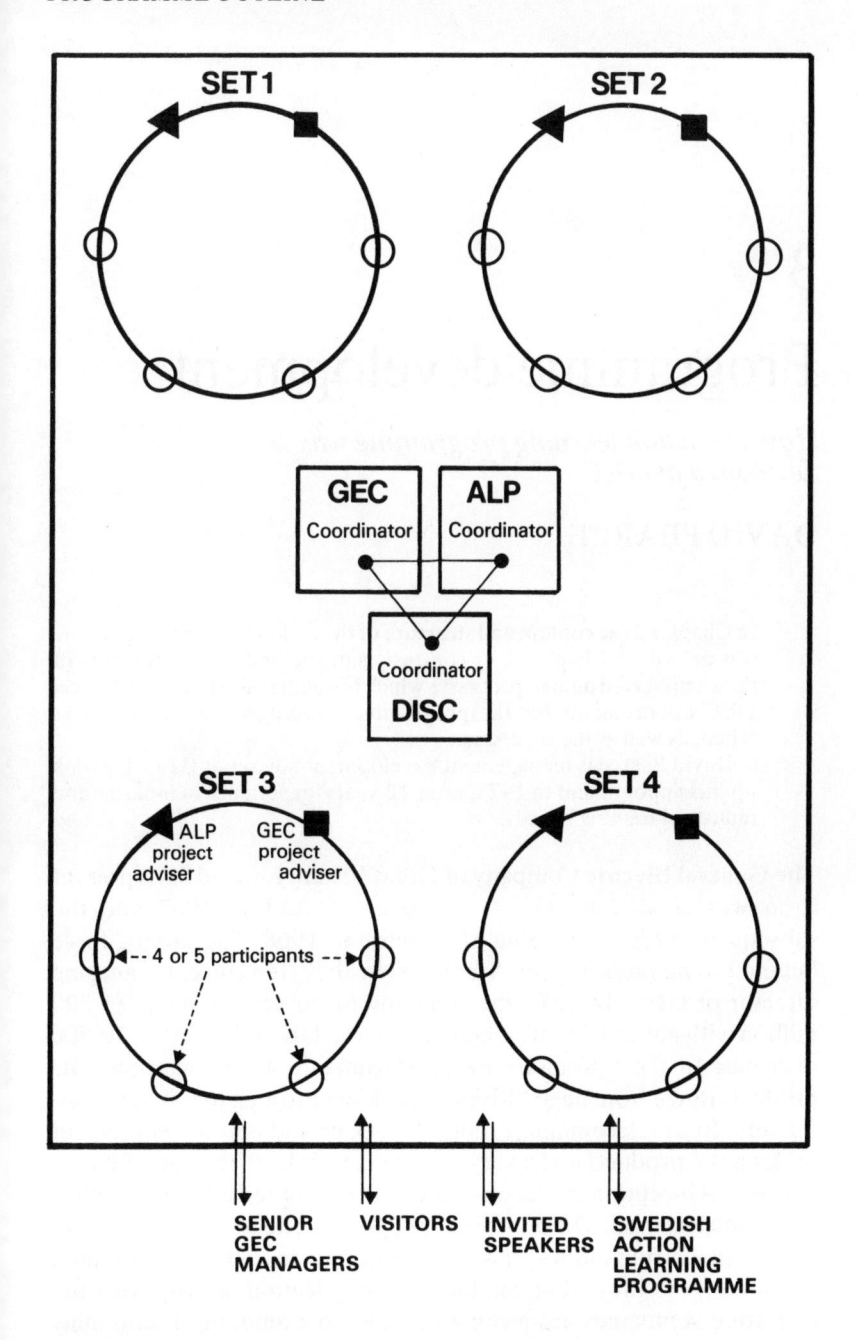

Figure 2 : 3 Composition of the learning community

3
Programme development

How the action learning programme was developed at GEC

DAVID PEARCE

> In Chapter 2 the content and structure of the action learning programme was described. Chapter 3, by contrast, is the behind-the-scenes story of the complicated human processes which brought it about. David Pearce, GEC's coordinator for the programme, describes some of the risks taken, as well as the successes.
>
> David Pearce is management development adviser at GEC. He took up this appointment in 1973, after 12 years' experience in industry and industrial training boards.

The General Electric Company of Great Britain Limited in its present form was created by GEC's takeover of AEI in 1967 and the subsequent merger with English Electric in 1968. The driving force behind the mergers was Sir Arnold Weinstock, the current managing director of GEC. In 1975 the company turnover was about £1 500 million with about 170 000 employees in the UK and a further 30 000 overseas. In the UK there are approximately 4 000 managers. Its products range from huge turbine generators through to tiny semiconductors; from telecommunications and space and defence equipment to domestic products and a very wide range of electrical equipment.

From its inception the reconstituted GEC adopted a vigorous policy of decentralization. The number of people at its head office has always been kept to a minimum — it is sometimes said, to a number who could comfortably fit into a London bus. The implication of this is that the operating companies are given a considerable amount of autonomy and require extremely capable business managers. The major unifying thread is the system of annual budgets which are discussed once a year in a face-to-face interview with Weinstock by the management team of each operating company. The regular monthly reporting of salient figures and business ratios provides the necessary feedback and control.

How the programme started

One of the earliest memos Sir Arnold sent to managing directors told them, among other things, not to send managers to business schools without his prior consent. In some quarters this was wrongly interpreted as meaning that management development was a taboo subject. During the five to six year period following the mergers Stanhope Gate (GEC's headquarters) concentrated its control effort on the business ratios.

By 1973 Sir Arnold was saying privately that he had spent five years creating one of the finest teams of managers in Western Europe, but that he wanted to ensure that the bulk of managers who were below his 'eye level' were being similarly trained. Concurrently Michael Bett had been in the personnel director's seat for just over a year and was attempting to steer the personnel function towards a broader role. An intensive industrial relations activity had been necessary during the rationalization period.

The development of managers had always been the responsibility of individual managing directors and remains so. However, business pressure did not always allow them to discharge this responsibility as systematically and vigorously as they would have wished. There was also a growing concern that good managers and technologists were being lost, because there was no way of ensuring that outstanding talent could be offered to another GEC company. The group as a whole was losing out as a result. Some of the operating companies were looking for a lead from the centre on the question of management development.

Sir Arnold had always been in favour of management development; indeed he saw his own role as primarily concerned with developing firstclass business managers. In November 1973 he saw a television programme in which Professor Revans outlined his theory of action learning and he decided that Mike Bett should explore, with the top people in the GEC operating companies, the applicability of setting up a management development programme based on action learning.

Designing the programme

From the outset it was made quite clear that the idea would have to stand or fall on its merits with the individual managing directors of the operating companies. The reactions were mixed, ranging from enthusiastic acceptance to sceptical rejection. Most were willing to give it a try. It was suggested by one managing director that his personnel director should visit Belgium and talk to the people who had been involved in the industry/university action learning programme run in Belgium for five or six years (see R. W. Revans, *Developing Effective Managers,* New York, Praeger Publishers, 1971). In the end, three of the personnel directors and I spent two days in Belgium in early 1974 discussing the programme with a wide selection of the people involved.

The result of the visit was acceptance of the action learning idea and a willingness to give it a try, provided that it was translated to meet the particular needs and style of GEC. Additionally it was questioned whether it was necessary for participants to spend as long as a year in a stranger-organization, as they did in Belgium. A shorter period was preferred.

Early in 1974 Professor Revans introduced a number of the directors from Action Learning Projects International (ALP) to GEC. ALP is a group of people from a variety of backgrounds, including the social services, nursing, local government, industry and academia. They had been meeting regularly for 18 months and were all very committed to the idea of action learning. This was the first major project which they had undertaken as a group, although all of them separately had carried out action learning work with Revans.

At an early stage in the relationship it was agreed that David Casey would act as the ALP coordinator of the GEC project and I was nominated as the GEC coordinator. Later John Teire came in as the coordinator for Dunchurch Industrial Staff College (DISC), a commercially run management training centre owned by GEC. Ray Godsall, the director of DISC, had already done some preliminary work for the GEC action learning management development programme. DISC was to be the centre for the programme, particularly during the formal course periods.

From the beginning it was clear that a great deal of trust was needed among the people organizing and operating the programme. In a conscious effort to develop the trust, all major issues were brought into the open and fully discussed. This was not time wasting (as it might have seemed to a casual observer). It paid dividends in achieving results. There were stages when the membership of this power group changed, depending on what was to be achieved, but it consisted at the very least of Mike Bett and the ALP and GEC coordinators. Professor Revans, Sir Arnold Weinstock, GEC senior managers — in particular the personnel directors — and subsequently the project advisers, all contributed at appropriate times.

Setting the pace

We had to decide whether to forge ahead at a rapid pace or whether to take things rather more slowly and, hopefully, do them better. In the end, we decided to produce practical results as quickly as possible. This led to the decision that the programme should be under way by October 1974 at the latest, approximately six months after the visit to Belgium.

It was necessary to move fast and we took a number of bold decisions. For example, the idea of using internal company project advisers was decided at such a late stage that three weeks of the programme had elapsed before the necessary agreement for one of the personnel directors' involvement could be obtained. Also the managers who put projects forward were given only the briefest indication of how the programme would operate and what would be expected of them. The effect of this neglect showed itself in the difficulties some of the participants had in obtaining the full confidence of their client.

None of us regrets the decision we took to go ahead quickly. We were convinced that action was necessary. We therefore decided to follow the basic tenets of action learning and have a go. Looking back we feel we have learned much faster this way and GEC is now running its third programme as this book goes to press.

GEC design and aims

At an early stage we wondered whether GEC should act as the catalyst to involve other major UK organizations in a consortium exchange programme serviced by academic institutions. It was quickly realized that this approach stood little chance of success in the short term, and that we would have to go it alone. However, it was hoped that other enterprises would cooperate by seconding managers to the programme as participants and by accepting GEC managers to undertake projects in their organizations. This was achieved with the Post Office and the Civil Service (see Chapters 5 and 6).

GEC's decentralized approach to running the company meant that the activity would only be able to go forward with the consent of the operating companies. There was no question of using pressure from Stanhope Gate. As a result not all operating companies decided to take part. Marrying GEC management philosophy and the philosophy of action learning produced the following working assumptions:

1. That experience itself is, or can be, a powerful instrument for developing managers.
2. That their development should aim to help them use their managerial experience in the most effective way.
3. That the reinterpretation and most effective use of past experience, from time to time assisted by fresh or additional knowledge gained through books, lectures or other traditional media, is best achieved by attempting to define and treat a real problem in real time in the real world.
4. That the conditions under which this problem is attacked should be such that all in the situation are able — if in varying degrees — to learn with and from each other.
5. That the role of the directing staff of the programme is therefore not to teach the participating managers but to provide the conditions in which the managers may themselves learn from the practical projects on which they are engaged.

On the operational front ideas were beginning to crystallize about the elements of the programme:

1. Significant business problems as projects.
2. Successful mid-career managers with potential as participants.
3. Regular meetings of the participants in small groups (project sets) aided by a project adviser.
4. A lengthy introductory, and mid-programme course.
5. The programme to be split into two parts, i.e. a diagnostic phase of project work, followed by an implementation phase.

The programme objectives gradually emerged clearly as the desire to:

1. Develop managers through the problems of the business and thereby improve the performance of the managers and the operation of the businesses.

2 Instigate a GEC-wide management development activity.
3 Test the method which appeared to be most suited to the operating ethos of GEC.
4 Accentuate the debate about management development within GEC and raise the issues to the surface.

Four options for participants

After considerable discussion it was decided that the programme should last about eight months, since it was felt that this was the maximum length of time the operating companies would countenance. A number of ways to involve participants developed and these are described in Appendix I.

Four options were developed because there was concern that secondment to another GEC operating company *(Option 1: Exchange between operating companies)* should not be the only way of undertaking the programme. Professor Charles Handy at London Business School brought it to a head by suggesting that some powerful 'barons' of organizations prefer to retain control of the development of their 'young Turks'. Out of this emerged the idea that an option should be offered which enabled a participant to undertake a project in another part of his own operating company, under the auspices of his own managing director *(Option 2: Remain in own GEC operating company)*.

The basic action learning logic was further extrapolated as follows. If the important element for learning is a real-time significant challenge, then surely a manager's day-to-day responsibilities provide this? So, why shouldn't an individual use his own job as his project? *(Option 3: Remain in own job)*. This option would be particularly useful to a manager just as he is taking up a new appointment, or to a manager who is coming to the end of a job and needs a gearchange in preparation for bigger responsibilities.

Lastly, we hoped for exchanges with other major UK companies, both in the engineering industry and outside it *(Option 4: Exchange with a non-GEC organization)*. For some time GEC's power engineering and telecommunications businesses had wanted to arrange exchanges and joint projects with their major customers, including some government departments. The action learning programme enabled links to be forged with the Post Office and the Civil Service. Exchanges with unrelated companies were not achieved this time, but in our second programme ICI and a trade union — the EETPU —

joined in, adding new dimensions to the learning of the whole community. Such cooperative ventures are helping to spread the practice of action learning in British organizations.

Criteria for participants

A lot of discussion took place about the qualities and qualifications needed by the candidates. It soon became apparent that businesses would have differing criteria and that the choice of candidates would have to be left to the individual managing directors of the businesses. The subsequent prospectus contained the following outline criteria for participants:

1 The participant should have proved his worth in a management or specialist job.
2 He should have the necessary potential for promotion (following completion of his programme) to senior general management — or to a specialist job leading to senior general management — within five years.
3 The participant must be convinced that the programme will assist significantly in his development as a manager.
4 The majority of participants are likely to be in their 30s, but age is less important than an individual's capacity to develop his management ability for the mutual advantage of himself and the company.

Criteria for projects

There was never any dispute that projects should be other than significant business problems to which the management of the company needed solutions, and was prepared to devote the necessary time and effort. However, no one was certain whether the businesses would be willing to reveal some of their more deepseated problems and subject them to the gaze of Stanhope Gate. The criteria for projects became:

1 The project should be concerned with a major business problem involving a broad understanding of the company. It should not be directed at the solution of problems which are exclusively technical.

PROGRAMME DEVELOPMENT

2 The project should cover more than one function of the business, requiring the involvement, cooperation and commitment of a number of managers.
3 The participant should spend approximately six to nine months working on the project. After initial agreement on his task, he would diagnose the problem, make recommendations and then help to initiate the necessary action. It is desirable but not necessary for the project to be capable of being completed within the time allowed.

The full prospectus

In addition to the criteria for projects and their participants many other considerations for programme design had to be debated before a start could be made. A brief prospectus was compiled and this proved to be a most useful document. Hundreds of copies of this prospectus were eventually needed, both inside and outside GEC, in order to communicate what the programme entailed. The original document is reproduced in Appendix I.

Relations between the organizers

The personnel department at Stanhope Gate was nominally in charge of the programme, assisted by the director of DISC. Revans was to be the overall architect. Although he was willing to devote as much time as necessary to selling, designing, and running the programme, his international commitments meant that he needed a representative who would handle it on a continuous basis. The solution was for ALP to form itself into a limited company and negotiate a contract with GEC. David Casey was nominated as the ALP coordinator and he took on the task of translating the swarm of excited ideas about the programme into a business contract. Eventually he created a big 'map' of the projected activity on one enormous piece of paper which showed the estimated requirements of the various components and the likely cost. From this a contract was drawn up between ALP and GEC for the provision of services, despite the fact that it was not totally clear what would eventually be involved. In the end an estimate was made and a solution agreed whereby ALP would run the formal courses, provide project advisers and have a major overall management role. The forecast proved very accurate in the end.

DISC, on the other hand, was accustomed to operating commercially. Its services and charges were known in the market place and those could easily be applied to the programme.

Obtaining participants

Managing directors were asked to submit names for the programme. At the same time negotiations were under way with outside organizations to see if they were willing to cooperate. Eventually 35 GEC candidates were put forward. It was arranged that they should be interviewed at Stanhope Gate by Revans and myself, assisted by other members of the personnel department. The purpose of the interview was to explain to each candidate the ethos of the programme and its emerging reality. It was made abundantly clear that this was not to be a programme to teach techniques, but an opportunity for each participant to accelerate his learning of the skills of managing in a real-life situation aided by the framework and elements of the programme. This was not to imply that management techniques would be completely ignored — aspects such as finance, organization and marketing were to be formally dealt with at various stages.

In the interview each candidate was talked through the programme to enable him to decide whether or not he wished to devote his efforts and time to it. This process was reinforced by asking him to go away and discuss with his wife and family the implications of spending eight months of his precious time and effort on the activity. A number of people decided that they didn't want to pursue it, some were promoted, others left GEC and one of the 35 was talked out of undertaking the programme because it was felt that he had not had sufficient management experience. One participant (David Carr) describes his own interview in Chapter 7. It was salutary for the interviewers to read how David Carr saw it.

Twenty-one participants eventually came under starter's orders, eighteen from GEC and three from the Post Office. During the programme one participant withdrew because of pressure of work in his company and another left GEC but has since returned. See Appendix III for a complete list of projects and participants.

Obtaining projects

Within GEC, managing directors were asked to submit suitable projects which were available in their businesses for visiting participants, using the criteria already established. Later there was to be a considerable debate about the difference between a problem, for which there is no known solution, and a puzzle, to which there is a solution after sufficient technical wrangling has been devoted to it. Much to everyone's surprise, 55 projects were put forward, of which the majority were suitable (although not all of them could be tackled).

Matching participants to projects

The matching of participants to projects started at the initial interviews. In each case an attempt was made to create a maximum mismatch between the candidate's previous experience and the demands of the project. If for example, the man had been a production manager all his life, he was offered projects concerned with the marketing and product policy side of the business. Once the type of project had been agreed, two or three were selected and offered to the potential participant. An introduction was then made for him to discuss the suggested project with the potential client. If they failed to reach agreement then he would be able to investigate his second choice. In practice, this alternative was never called on — agreement was reached in every case with the first company approached. Others who were doing their 'own-job' option had readymade situations.

ALP project advisers

ALP had contracted to provide the necessary project advisers to service the eventual number of project sets. It was agreed with GEC that they needed to be people of stature and ability. The most important criterion was that they should have had experience of working with small groups helping them to maximize their learning from situations. Additionally it was expected that they would have a grasp of industry and the broader commercial and political scene. ALP was able to produce very quickly a list of a dozen such people. This was eventually reduced to the required four.

David Casey, an independent consultant, was to add the role of project adviser to that of ALP coordinator. Jean Lawrence, another director of ALP and a senior consultant at Manchester Business School, joined him. Tony Eccles, then a senior lecturer at Manchester Business School and now professor of business policy at Glasgow

University, made the third. Bob Garratt, another independent, came into the team from the Architectural Association and various activities in the management education field in the UK and Northern Ireland.

GEC project advisers

From the outset Revans had always implied that GEC should stand on its own feet as quickly as possible. Much later David Casey brought us face to face with the reality of what this meant by a written statement which said 'ALP International politely but firmly refuses to play any part in the second programme'. This meant that GEC would need to be able to provide its own project advisers for future programmes. Revans wrote a paper, 'On the choice of internal project advisers', to highlight the situation. It was now a fairly late stage in the preparations. Initially line managers were considered as possibles, but eventually we decided it should be personnel people, and if possible personnel directors of the operating companies. This immediately raised the question of their availability to spend at least one day a week with the project sets and a substantial amount of formal course time, up to five weeks in all. Nigel Eldred, personnel director of GEC Power Engineering, and James Pease-Watkin, personnel director of GEC-Marconi, agreed to undertake the task. Glyn Trollope, GEC's group personnel manager, also accepted the challenge. Glyn writes of his experience in the role in Chapter 14. John Shrigley, the personnel director of Electrical Components, was to come in later.

The introduction of the GEC project advisers was one of the most significant decisions in setting up the programme. They added and reinforced the GEC operating style during the programme and provided a sounding board which ensured that the activity was keyed into the company. The benefits of this were readily seen when setting up the second programme; the idea has been adopted in the Indian Nehru Project.

Building project sets

We decided to form project sets before the programme started, where possible five to six weeks in advance, so that project advisers would be able to make contact with their participants and the clients, and hold preliminary meetings of their sets before the first formal session in October. In fact, project sets were not actually formed until two weeks before the beginning of the programme. Up to the moment that the programme started there were still so many variables that it was difficult to finalize them. At a certain point we took the decision that the four project sets would be formed on the known information available, and that adjustments would have to come later.

In order to introduce as much variety as possible into each set, a range of factors was taken into account. Participants exercising various options (as described in Appendix I) were shared amongst the sets, as were the accountants, the production men and the marketing men. The three participants from non-GEC organizations were studiously assigned to different sets. Finally, the types of projects were also mixed as much as possible.

The maximum number of participants per set was to be six with five as the optimum. Each set was assigned an external project adviser for the duration of the programme. Each set naturally developed its own life style and there was little call for transfers from one to another. None actually took place.

The two residential periods

In the Belgian programme the introductory course had always been of six to eight weeks' duration. This seemed to us far too long in a programme based upon responsible action. Revans at once agreed that it could be reduced, since one reason for the long period in Belgium was because of the strong university say in the management of their programme. In fact Revans was forthright in his view that it could be very considerably shortened. The outcome was a two and a half week period at the beginning and one week at the mid-point.

Client involvement

It was realized very early that the clients were as important a group as the participants. In ideal circumstances the clients would have been brought together very frequently, with a formal activity at the outset. The reality of the situation, because they were all very busy managers, prevented this happening so that compromises had to be worked out. It was realized that their support for the particular participant and the project set was vital. Consequently two days were set aside towards the end of the first three weeks to invite clients to DISC to talk through the project and the programme. This was completely organized by the participants themselves and it was noticeable that after a period of sweaters and jeans we were back to formal business suits to ensure that the clients felt that they were on home ground. Throughout the programme clients were regularly involved in project set meetings, often at their own factories. However, many of the participants spent a great deal of time getting the ear of their clients, who sometimes changed at various stages throughout the project. It became clear that the clients are as important as the participants and must be formally written into future programmes.

Involvement of senior management

Senior managers were invited to the programme at strategic points, particularly during the February course when programme participants wanted to discuss with them how they managed their businesses. These exchanges with managing directors were very useful and informative. Sir Arnold came as well. The process leading up to his visit created a great deal of excitement, speculation and tension. In the event everyone was extremely impressed by the brilliance and humanity of the man.

Re-entry

To all the participants the return to their organizations on completion of the programme was a major concern. The jobs of most exchange participants had been filled as soon as they had left them. To these men their next job became an increasingly important topic from the mid-point course onward. Some were to return to their own companies and others eventually found jobs in different parts of GEC. The process of fitting man and job was a strenuous and anxious activity for everyone involved — individuals' careers were at stake!

On the other hand, the own-job participants were by definition still holding the same positions in their companies. In a number of cases their trauma was to come to fruition after the end of the programme, when they became starkly aware of their newly acquired skills and abilities and were not always able to persuade their management to use them to best advantage — at least not in the short-term!

We learned a lot about the re-entry process from this first experience. It is a vital issue which needs to be in the organizers' minds from the very first planning meeting. Firstly, the senior managers who nominate a participant can be encouraged to talk through with their nominee the reasons for putting him forward, and the kind of plans which are being made for his future. The participant, for his part, should be encouraged to see himself (in marketing terms) as a product which has to be sold. During the programme each participant will acquire new strengths, knowledge, skills, abilities and insights which he will want to be able to illustrate to prospective buyers — whether strangers or longstanding colleagues. In future, time should be deliberately set aside at the beginning of the programme to allow participants to collect data about their own existing managerial performance. Such information would enable each participant to check and verify for himself the changes in his own behaviour.

Re-entry is the eternal problem of management educators and trainers. With action learning programmes it is quite possible — in fact absolutely essential — to continue the learning and support phase during re-entry. At a minimum it can be tackled by holding a number of project set meetings after the participants have taken up their new positions.

The management development debate continues

The contributions in this book give a bird's eye view of the tensions and excitement of the programme as seen by the people intimately involved in it. A lot was learned which is steadily being applied, but a lot of the important issues remain. They crystallized vividly quite early on — in fact just two months after the programme began. One evening there was a meeting at which the ALP and GEC project advisers and the programme coordinators heatedly discussed management development, action learning, DSMP 1 and GEC.

There was certainly no consensus, but it was possible to put together, after this long and intensive discussion, some notes as a record for ourselves, which are included in Appendix II. We felt at the time a great exhilaration as the debate ranged over a wide and difficult series of fundamental issues. And the debate continues, spreading in an ever-widening ripple, secure in the knowledge that at the very least it is founded on the healthy reality of action.

Part Two
Participants' experiences

A full list of participants and their projects will be found in Appendix III, page 139

4
The project is everything

A micro-electronics product policy problem tackled by a manager from another part of GEC

BILL PRINCE

> Bill Prince is the assistant divisional manager of GEC Mobile Radio Division. He graduated in engineering at Birmingham University, and then trained at Metropolitan Vickers. Before his present appointment he held manufacturing posts in the GEC companies at Henley and Walsall.

This is an account of the effect that various parts of the action learning programme had on me as a participant, concentrating on the effects of the project itself. In such a self-examination there are obvious risks. It may be difficult for a person to examine his own thoughts and actions with unprejudiced detachment and honesty. There is also the possibility that immediate effects are subtle and unmeasurable, maturing only in combination with further experiences long after the action learning programme has finished. Accepting these risks, I feel that it is possible to think about my own reactions to the various stimuli; otherwise this chapter would not have been written. Indeed I think that it is an important part of the learning process that a participant should engage in this kind of rumination.

I do not believe that this type of programme produces a 'before' and 'after' man, but it develops a keener ability to think about the political and personal forces between working managers as well as the actual business problems which they are facing, and particularly to see where one's own influences feature inside these relationships. And so I see the programme as producing a sort of reference point for personal development, a trig point based upon which the map of experience can be made more relevant.

And so one of the first tangible effects of the programme appeared to be a break from present responsibilities, but of course the more senior these responsibilities the greater the risk of taking that break. Having said that, the break had to be made, particularly since I am a great believer in management rotation to keep bringing fresh minds to bear on an organization and to prevent reactions being dulled by continual exposure to problems which can in time be accepted as insoluble. There was risk. For the individual participant there was the lurking possibility of having to return to the same level of responsibility after the break. When matters of strategy and policy at inter-company level have been tackled in the programme, it could be very stifling to go back to managing a single function.

The project

Previous manufacturing management experience had given me a thorough involvement with management accounts and budgetary control and I had been deeply involved with personnel activities. Even so my original qualification and continuing interest was in engineering and I was keen to increase the technical content of my work. I therefore deliberately chose a project based on high technology, namely advanced electronic components. The project was to establish the product policy for the company. This would cause me to grapple with the problems of a company using technology with which I had no previous experience.

I found that the technology and applications were not difficult to appreciate. On the other hand, the intangible problems of strategy and judgement which the managing director had to face, competing in an industry which operated on an international scale and which was often at the frontiers of technology, were tremendously baffling.

I galloped into the project picking up the surface problems, initially seeing the solution in a more comprehensive and better disciplined production control system; there was something fundamentally wrong with the layout of the unit; the unit needed a more comprehensive selling activity. Then I began to realize that these were popular 'cure-all' solutions. There were deeper problems which needed to be faced. They were much more difficult to describe and could only be discussed when a certain degree of trust had been built up. But until these matters had been recognized, no amount of attention to surface problems would produce any significant benefit.

What I was digging down to was the question of how a group of people operated together — how their personalities balanced, which one was

THE PROJECT IS EVERYTHING

the outcast, and how these relationships were fundamental to the way in which the whole company operated. This effect was even greater in a high technology company where the management style was more liberal than in other more autocratic companies in which I had worked.

I was also seeing effects which I recognized with great clarity from my own previous experiences. I was recognizing from time to time in other people reactions that I would have felt, stances I would have taken, and I saw the effect for good or ill of such actions. Was this a deliberate part of the exercise? I don't know, but the spotlight was turning back on to myself.

Three very fruitful learning situations had now shown themselves. Firstly, the way in which a problem continually redefines itself as you strip off the surface layers and dig deeper into the pressures and politics of the mix of people that make up a business. Secondly, the way in which this type of project can be used as a mirror to reveal strengths and weaknesses in yourself which you see in other people. Thirdly, by studying a company with a completely different business, fundamental problems can be recognized with tremendous clarity which are common to most businesses.

Was my project real?

The basis of an action learning programme is that a real-life situation is used for learning. But is it real life? It is very real in that you are completely alone inside a company to formulate your own approach, to work at a pace set by yourself, to decide for yourself how to overcome political problems. Also, as the majority of participants are GEC staff working inside GEC companies, the pressure to produce real results is very high. In any case of conflict the search for tangible results took precedence over the learning process. When we met the participants from a Belgian programme who were working in different companies we detected a more relaxed atmosphere and a greater tendency to look on the project as an educational exercise. In retrospect, I think it was right for a GEC 'results' type pressure to be felt since this was the normal working environment and in this respect the projects were 'real life'.

In another sense the projects were slightly artificial since participants were insulated from the normal political currents. The participants were therefore able to discuss situations with people inside and outside the company in a way not possible for the managing director or other managers involved inevitably through history, seniority and accountability. Almost without exception people eventually unwound and confided their worries, frustrations and their constructive proposals in a way that would not have been possible if I had been part of the permanent hierarchy.

Was the project real or artificial? It combined the best of both worlds. The real-life pressure was there for results and as an exercise in pacing oneself and self-starting. The problems encountered in the business were real and immediate. However, there was a privileged relationship which allowed a deeper, more detached, basis for discussion with many of the key people involved.

The project as a business exercise

As well as disentagling the political influences it was instructive to use the project as a business case study. Every business thinks that it has the product with the most baffling stock control problem, the most unreasonable customers, the most intractable technical problems and the toughest competition. The company I joined was no exception but being a stranger to the product and to the technology allowed me to look right inside the workings with eyes untrammelled by short-term problems and to recognize symptoms common across companies irrespective of product.

I was often speaking to relatively junior personnel who could see very clearly serious problems in their own vicinity and elsewhere in the company. Either their supervisors could not see them because they were too close to the problem, or perhaps they could see them and were avoiding action. A junior employee does care about the fortunes of the company he works in; he does not complicate issues with history, politics or obscure accountancy theory. A junior employee often sees and defines problems with far more clarity than more senior managers. Were these problems also present in the company I came from? Of course they were. That was one reason why they could be recognized, why they stood out as familiar factors in a foreign landscape. In many cases they underlined problems which I had not fully appreciated in the company I had left. The mirror effect was working again.

Being in foreign surroundings where you have no pretensions to being an expert in designing, making or selling the product, makes it very easy to ask the idiot questions. It is amazing how often the simple question is difficult to answer, touches a nerve, and sometimes produces a solution.

When you are directly involved in running a company or a department there is a sort of ostrich effect which assumes that current problems will disappear; the orders will turn up magically; the crushing technical problem which has been with us for several months will be solved next period; we will suddenly be able to recruit the specialist labour that has not previously been available.

My host company had some of these problems. It did have a severe recruiting problem and it was difficult to see a magic cure. It did have a tremendous amount at stake on a single customer whose product was subject to severe technical problems and an unpredictable demand pattern. It was subject to very strong political pressures from the parent company.

One challenge which I faced was the extent to which I could communicate the real problems of this company in a diplomatic way to parts of GEC beyond the immediate management, to enlist the powerful help of those outside the company. My project in its fullest sense was drawn far beyond the confines of the specific company I was working in. Although I learned a lot about these external political forces and how they affect the way a company runs, I feel that I was not able to exert any discernible influences in this area.

Lessons learned from the diagnosis phase

And so a number of lessons come through. The power of simple fundamental questions. The fact that a fundamental problem does not disappear however sophisticated the method by which it is measured. The fact that problems are usually recognized with stark clarity somewhere inside the organization, and usually not at the highest level of management. The fact that the operation of a company inside a group is affected to a great extent by political forces external to itself and not always in a rational or helpful way.

From analysis to implementation

In an action learning programme the work of diagnosis is only the first step and it is necessary to move on to the more difficult activities of constructive proposals and implementation. Destructive criticism can be useful shock treatment to create a reaction upon which some course of action can be built, but the timing has to be just right. At the wrong moment it can put a project back if confidences and relationships have to be rebuilt after being shattered by wrong timing. In general people react badly to destructive criticism, they have heard it before, often they feel it is true but feel powerless to deal with it. What people are looking for is reassurance and constructive proposals.

When considering implementation one is not able to change the labour force, change the supervision, change the industry or the government! It is necessary to search out the good and build on that, not to parade the bad and thoroughly depress oneself and the people amongst whom one is working. It is easy enough for a group of people to convince themselves that action in the face of severe problems is futile. Normally the necessary actions are already being considered somewhere in the company but action is blocked by frustrations, by lack of universal acceptance across the company, or by lack of conviction by the manager concerned. These commitments have to be searched out, unlocked and welded together as a practical course of action.

Was I successful in this aspect of my project? It was relatively easy to recognize the vital issues. It was fairly easy to create a platform for those issues to be discussed and placed on record as an agreed company document. It was much harder to achieve action in line with proposals agreed by all as relevant and necessary. Only time will tell to what extent my method of working inside the company was effective. Very often I felt as though I was introducing people inside the company to each other and getting them to share rather than offload a problem. It is perhaps this act of creating an atmosphere of cohesion, a unity of purpose which is the fundamental management task. The relearning of this fact and practice, however successful in its achievement, emerges as a tremendously important content of the action learning programme.

The project develops my sensitivity

The project turned out to be a very effective means of getting to know about myself. One of the most powerful realities was the complete isolation in the project. General management can be a very lonely business and the project recreates this feeling. Relieved of day-to-day responsibilities, I had no escape to busyness in times of stagnation. The project was always there and it became very important to feel that progress was being made. I got used to thinking about my progress and pacing myself. At times I felt tremendous pressure from those I was working with, pressure brought to bear by their expectations of the wonder solution. Why else was I there? During my first week or so people responded well and were impressed by my ability to see the

THE PROJECT IS EVERYTHING

surface problems, but as time passed, they expected me to be able to dig deeper, to be able to discuss deeper and more fundamental truths about the industry in general and the company in particular. And at times when I was not able to respond, I got used to detecting the glazed expression, the polite acceptance of my views without reaction.

This was a crucial point in the exercise and I learned to interpret the warning signs, to change the approach, to maintain interest and to develop techniques to sustain the positive reaction necessary to get inside people's deeper thoughts and motives. All these pressures were developing inside me rather than being applied from outside as disciplines, and in retrospect the lessons learnt were more complete and lasting because of this.

Any political situation in a company is the meeting and balancing of a mix of personalities. In searching for solutions to problems people look firstly to a comfortable surface effect, such as changing the layout of an office or machine shop, or altering a paperwork system. The next hunting ground for a solution lies in the activities and attitudes of various people in the company, *other* people in the company. Only when trust and respect have been established will these other people be ready to discuss how they themselves operate, and possibly be prepared to debate their own failures. My experience is that it is normally easy to achieve this type of dialogue. A more difficult challenge is to build upon the opportunity in a way that gets each person to recognize what he is saying. This is the surest way to achieve a modified approach for the future, but it is important that this type of intimate discussion does not put up barriers in the relationship being fostered.

This proved to be a very fruitful learning part of the project. Achieving this type of relationship and also exploiting it in a helpful way is a skill which requires continuous practice and development. It is the skill which gets you inside your contact's thought processes, attitudes, fears and vanities. These processes are often understood by recognizing elements of one's own attitudes and vanities; hopefully this leads to a modification of one's own approach.

The set was of very limited help to me

I have not previously discussed the operation of the set, in which four participants worked jointly away from the project location. Different sets operated in different ways; one set was strong in a disciplined approach and drove the project work along by demanding progress reports and achievement of tangible targets in each other's project work. Another set got involved deeply in the intricacies of each other's project work. Our own set tended to do neither of these; rather it almost went through the programme searching for a formula for operation. If it did have a style it was scrutiny of the approach which we were each making to carry out our project. It was a wall of cotton wool against which we each in turn tried to make an impression, selling ourselves or our project or digging to find help or a clue to a useful course of action when we returned to our project. I do not consider that I found any help with the project from the set. The neutrality of the set heightened the feeling of loneliness and isolation in the project and probably, by contrast, increased the realness of this pressure and learning. If I had to think of a benefit from the set meetings, it would probably have nothing to do with the project work. It would probably be with the guidance and organization of a group of equal partners without any focal point for authority, a common enough situation in say a trade association, or when carrying out a coordinating role in a company outside the normal hierarchy.

In contrast, the project probably had by far its greatest and hopefully most lasting effect in the subtle areas, highlighting my own abilities and characteristics and establishing in a fairly clinical way how these could be made effective in various situations. I would put the value of these lessons very high as foundation blocks for self-development to continue as a normal part of my everyday approach to work.

What it leaves behind

Inevitably, the programme in its tangible form comes to an end. The transition of participants back to normal responsibilities still needs further study. Having to cope with the dramas and uncertainties of re-establishing myself back into a normal responsibility at the same time as finishing off the project meant that the project had to take second place behind the more compelling priority of my own personal future. This was a waste that was difficult to pardon.

This lack of activity in the administrative arrangements could well be because some of the real effects of the programme had been underestimated. I found that having tasted blood as it were in the realms of company policy, having practised the disentanglement of political situations in their own right, I was impatient to exploit these skills in a challenging post.

Yes, the course had produced an increase in self-confidence, a recognition that there were still fresh challenges to meet and some insight into approaches that could be used to meet those challenges. Approaches and techniques that did not come from books, lectures or even tutorials, but in seeking out and applying one's already existing qualities and experience. The fact that these abilities were found to exist already and did not have to be synthesized in some contrived way makes them far more powerful and makes the urge to get on and use them that more urgent.

What of the future? It will need the passage of several years before a further chapter can be written to test the relevance and lasting results of the experience, but the impact feels very powerful now.

5

Learning how to learn

Participants from the Post Office and GEC work together

PETER PRESTON

> Peter Preston is an executive engineer within the Telecommunications headquarters of the Post Office Corporation. In recent years he has been mostly concerned with the materials aspects of electronic components. He is a member of the Institute of Physics.
>
> His coparticipant on the project, Peter Howard, is a manager in the printed circuits division of GEC Telecommunications Ltd at Coventry.

Before the start of the GEC action learning programme I had accepted that one learnt by doing things (rather than by being told how to do things), but did not realize that management could be taught in this way. Although previous experience had given me opportunity of considerable involvement with equipment suppliers, component manufacturers and research establishments, both at home and abroad, the action learning programme seemed an ideal chance to gain further experience at the manufacturing end of the business. But my decision to join was not taken lightly. I had reservations about being used as a guineapig in an experimental training programme with an apparently vague curriculum. There was considerable risk in accepting a role where one was expected to act 'entirely upon one's own responsibility' but in an investigation involving a potentially sensitive area in manufacturer-customer relations (both commercially and technically). There was also the possibility, however remote, of the programme containing little of lasting value.

I accepted the opportunity and left my job for the duration of the programme on the understanding that I would return to it afterwards.

The first few weeks of the programme were different from previous management training courses which I had attended. I found it generally uncomfortable, often confusing and at times downright irritating. It was difficult as a non-GEC participant with a predominantly technical background to feel at home in what appeared an overwhelming commercial atmosphere. My feelings could not be explained solely by the unfamiliar surroundings, as in changing jobs from one company to another or between divisions within the same company. In these circumstances tasks and objectives are reasonably well defined and in line with the overall strategy of the business. My position did not seem nearly so clearly defined. I had a straight and difficult path to negotiate and anticipated all sorts of pressures which would tend to deflect me from that path. This does not mean that I was not openminded nor that I had prejudged the outcome of our project investigation. Nevertheless I had clearly been pitched in at the deep end. Upon reflection this was an effective introduction to action learning, but a more thorough preparation on my part and the knowledge that my own organization understood and appreciated the position in which I had been placed, would have helped.

Not all of the initial residential course affected me in that way. The lectures stimulated quite a lot of thought. More time could have been devoted to discussion of their content, particularly after we had had time to relate some of the points to situations which developed within our projects.

At the end of the residential course I needed time to review my position, collect my thoughts and discuss a few difficulties with respected colleagues. I see now that the proper place for this should have been within our project set group, but at the time I was not ready to do this and I do not think that there was sufficient cohesion in our group to have handled the problem helpfully.

I was not the only participant with mixed feelings about taking part. Some people seemed to be having difficulty in finding enough time to attend meetings, let alone tackle project work. Others, working on their projects singlehanded, were more alone than I was. They were not only in different companies but also looking at problems well outside their usual fields of work. At least I was one of a joint investigation team investigating a familiar subject.

Joint working

Working in a two-man team provided the opportunity for immediate discussions on issues as and when they developed in project work. Had more time been available to my partner, very rapid progress could have been made in these investigations. The unequal availability of time was the single biggest drawback of our arrangement. I felt that it was not proper to press on with some project work in isolation from my partner, since this may have resulted in his missing such a lot of the learning process and there could have been a lack of commitment on his part in the final analysis. At times the sympathy that we both felt for each other's situation was tested to the limit.

When compared with singlehanded projects I would guess that the advantages and disadvantages of the joint arrangement would make a premeditated choice for one or the other a matter of taste. When investigations cross the boundaries of two organizations, it certainly does help to have a person from each company taking part as a combined venture. This minimized problems of introduction into the organizations and saved time by knowing where to go and who to see. The past experience of both of us could be brought to bear in solving problems and this was particularly helpful since this experience tended to be complementary rather than similar. Another benefit was the opportunity that we had to study each other's perceptions of the underlying causes of problems, and to analyse how these had been influenced by our previous experience and the type of business in which our views had been formed. I imagine that we all make mental assessments of the motives of others in work situations, but rarely do we get the opportunity to test these judgements in an atmosphere of honest confidentiality and in the interests of mutual understanding and development.

The joint arrangement probably had more to commend it from a learning point of view than from the point of view of actually solving a business problem. There are few solutions to problems which are ideal for both manufacturer and customer, particularly when the customer is one of several purchasers of that manufacturer's goods. Nevertheless, I was surprised at exactly how much progress and agreement was possible with sufficient will to overcome problems. Some form of compromise is probably the only solution acceptable to both parties and it may only be possible to debate the issues involved, offer alternative actions and their possible consequences, and leave the final course of action to each enterprise. This in itself can be of considerable help to the client since it provides an illumination of the problem in depth. It does, however, limit the opportunity for the participants of complete action learning, by restricting the implementation phase.

My understanding of the singlehanded project is that it is a much more lonely experience. In this respect it represents more accurately the situations encountered in senior management. The project set provides a shelter from this isolation to a much greater degree than it does in the paired arrangement and it becomes more important for the group to provide support. The overriding advantage of the single-handed project is the personal freedom to proceed at one's own pace and with uncompromised responsibility. The risks may be greater but the credit for success is probably more rewarding.

Value to me

One of the most frustrating aspects of an action learning programme is the common lack of understanding, among those not involved, of what participation was intended to achieve. There seems to be an obsession with the outcome of the project, as though that was the only value from the investment of a participant for the nine months period. Had the programme been designed to instruct in particular skills such as production control or inflation-accounting, or to solve a unique set of business problems, it could be argued that there were more effective and less expensive ways of going about it. A major value of the programme is the experience and learning gained by the participants. The utility of a successfully completed project — and this can be considerable — is still not as valuable as the potential of the participant calculated over the rest of his working career. This experience cannot be passed on to a third party.

The project is the vehicle for learning. The project set meetings were of particular importance since they offered me the opportunity to study other facets of the business scene with which I had no previous experience. The diversity of projects enabled me to obtain an insight into the full width of a business. Through discussions it was possible to make a real contribution to the solution of problems completely outside my own particular discipline. I was intrigued by how often it was possible for a nonexpert to make valuable contributions by applying basic principles rather than specialized knowledge. Project set meetings were not occasions for remote interest, they offered unique opportunities for involvement in commercial issues of which I had no firsthand experience. I learnt that there is a difference between sitting on the outside of a problem and being involved to the degree that a moral responsibility is taken for actions.

Project work also provided access to many senior people within both organizations. The invitation of managing directors to the courses extended this opportunity much wider than would have been possible under normal circumstances — at least in the same period of time. Apart from the value of listening to their views on how businesses work, the experience of sustained exposure to these minds had a maturing effect.

Nine months' involvement in an action learning programme is not likely to guarantee the development of the perfect manager, nor does it give the participant the right to lecture others. However, the experience helped us to understand what differentiates good management from inferior management. Certain qualities demonstrated by successful managers stood out as an example to others and these rarely included in-depth knowledge of academic skills.

These qualities include awareness, particularly awareness of the constantly changing influences acting upon and attempting to deflect the course of planned actions, and the sensitivity to detect from these influences the need for adjustment to thinking and actions. Adaptability is required to respond quickly and decisively. And above all, courage is needed to admit that change is necessary when confronted with this evidence. The unwillingness to admit that previous judgements were wrong often impedes the objectivity needed to take the right decision. Poor understanding of objectives and their relationship to overall company purpose may be a primary cause of error.

Learning, for me, can be classified into two categories. The first involves the learning of facts. The second stems from experience, and fashions the way in which we respond to events in the future. I have learned many facts from my participation in the programme. This was inevitable when undertaking an investigation in depth under such circumstances. I also feel more capable to respond to situations in the future — as a result of the second type of learning — through greater awareness and an understanding of the things that it would be more prudent for me to learn. A benefit of action learning principles is that their application does not finish at the conclusion of the organized programme but they become an essential part of the process of continuous personal development.

6
This is the way to unlock resources

A GEC manager is assigned to a major problem in a government department

DON HOWELL

> Don Howell is finance manager, GEC Power Engineering Ltd. He obtained a degree in mechanical engineering at Imperial College, London, and then qualified as a chartered accountant with a City firm. He spent five years as a management consultant before joining GEC Turbine Generators Ltd in April 1973, where he worked on the manufacturing side until the action learning programme.

If you think that journeying into the unknown can provide one of the most effective learning experiences then you will probably agree that I had the best opportunity on the whole programme. Not only did I leave my own job and my own company but I left the GEC Group and landed in a major department of the Civil Service. My project was on planning. The Official Secrets Act does not allow me to go into details, but during my seven months' stay I had to conduct a series of in-depth explorations back into major private sector companies to research current practice. The objective was to help the department take action on the basis of the information gathered.

My colleagues on the programme seemed to know little more than I did about planning in the formal sense — particularly when related to huge organizations with their inherent inertia. In general, the textbooks were not up-to-date; the state of the art had moved forward rapidly to combat the uncertainty of the real world in recent years. The fact that I was unable to lean on anyone forced me to get down to first principles in evaluating and comparing the information from the private sector companies. Without the inevitable prejudices which the planning expert would have had, I was able to sort out quickly the more valuable principles and was probably less inhibited in asking the question which might have been too obvious for the expert but which, in practice, produced a revealing answer.

The department regarded the project as extremely important and was eager for its completion. This leads me to an important conclusion. The project *must* be of vital importance to the host organization. The client must be committed to its successful conclusion. No one will learn much from a project which has been dreamed up for an action learning programme except, perhaps, not to dream again!

The value of the set

I learned a lot from the actual project, both from its technical content and from firsthand experience of how the Civil Service operates. But although these were valuable personal benefits the more significant learning experience for me came from the project set.

All the participants in our set — and advisers as well — looked forward greatly to the one day per week meetings at which we exchanged experiences not only on our projects but also on a thousand other subjects. Motivation, changing attitudes, participation, world economics, these and many more topics came up for challenging debate. No quarter was given nor expected in the discussion and it is interesting to reflect now how much the input of energy and enthusiasm contributed to the learning experience. Above all else we learned how to help one another. The set became a very efficient problem-solving unit — we seemed to be so much more powerful as a unit than the sum of our individual resources would suggest. Much of this was due to the composition of the set and its size. We were never more than seven — four participants and up to three advisers. Our personalities and backgrounds, in terms of education, experience, jobs, professional qualifications and personal circumstances, were very different. We concluded that the optimum size for discussion groups on this type of exercise is about five to seven.

Benefits

The potential benefit to GEC of the action learning concept is enormous. Making this statement twelve sobering months after the completion of the programme, I can hardly be accused of having a euphoric 'end of term' spirit. Most of the analysis has, perhaps naturally, concentrated on the benefits to participants as individuals and to a lesser degree the benefits to GEC of the projects. But I believe the principle of action learning is the key to unlocking resources which, for a number of reasons, have been under-utilized in solving our problems. These resources exist at all levels.

We really can, as Professor Revans says, help each other more and teach ourselves through reorganizing our experience. Over and over again in my own work I am now taking the opportunity to encourage managers to learn from each other. In the last few years the idea of pooling experiences and sharing insights may have been swamped in the general rush for autonomy. Managers have been measured principally on their own business results, whilst the contribution they could make to the benefit of their colleagues has been neglected.

The participants on the programmes are now acting as catalysts in different parts of the Group, using action learning principles in the day-to-day running of businesses. We reinvent the wheel less frequently and obtain more effective use of our resources. When the sum of these effects is taken into account the investment on the programmes in terms of time and money must be minuscule in comparison with the benefits to the business.

7
It didn't work for me

A manager tries to take on his own job as an action learning project

DAVID CARR

> David Carr has spent all of his career at the English Electric Valve Company Ltd, having held a number of engineering posts before his present appointment as a divisional manager. He started by taking a natural sciences degree at Cambridge.

I had joined my company direct from Cambridge 14 years before. During these years reading and personal experience had given me prejudices about management training. Our local senior management did not encourage formal management training, although they sponsored engineers for MSc or PhD degrees in technical subjects. With specialized departments to help them with personnel, accounting and commercial problems, engineers did not need general management courses. We grew our managers in our many separate product departments. Despite this lack of encouragement, a number of my colleagues had taken three-year evening courses at the local technical college. The company had paid their expenses, but they did not become managers any more quickly just because they had been on a course.

In my company there were suspicions that head office was not keen on management training — too expensive and academic. Consultants had also come in for some stick from GEC headquarters. All things considered, a pretty inauspicious start.

IT DIDN'T WORK FOR ME

Introduction to the programme

When my managing director invited me to take part in the programme, the description given to me was scanty, probably because he was incompletely briefed. Each participant would be given a project, a problem in his own or another GEC company, to study. He and other participants would meet in groups once a week to help each other with their problems. It would take nine months and cost the company £2 500 per participant. My first reaction to the cost was to ask: 'Could I have a dozen rotary vacuum pumps instead?' I was assured that I could have them too. There would be an interview at GEC head office and, in preparation for this, I should write a letter to the personnel department there saying what benefits I expected to get from the programme.

This put me in a quandary. I had had a very short briefing; I did not believe in management training but was being asked to say how good it would be for me. It brought back a vivid memory of school where I was given as an imposition an essay on a religious subject with the assumption that I was a believer. Being an unbeliever I could not bring pen to paper and had to volunteer for a detention instead.

In the event, I wrote some words to the effect that British industry had amply demonstrated its managerial incompetence so that we could not learn much from each other, but should look together at how other nations did better.

Early meetings

The interview at head office with Reg Revans and David Pearce was a rather overawing occasion until it got under way. I was pleasantly surprised to find such congenial people — head offices can be pretty offputting places.

Looking back, I do not remember being told much in detail about the programme I was about to join. Perhaps they thought I was already briefed or pehaps they were not certain themselves. I referred to my letter, but they were not able to put their hand on it! I explained that I did not think we could learn much from each other within British industry, but should look to see why businesses did better abroad. I was particularly impressed by the European electrical giants like Thomson, Siemens and Philips. They did not show much profit and thus avoided taxation, but managed to spend generously on finding new products and keeping their plant modern. I understood that Philips used current cost accounting which gave them bigger depreciation charges and a smaller but sounder profit. Reg Revans' comment was that I should join the programme if I wanted to spread this sort of seditious message. He also promised to arrange a meeting with some of the participants on the Belgian programme.

David Pearce indicated some of the other possible participants and some of the proposed projects to be matched against them. He promised to send some notes on the form of the programme, hoped I would be joining it and sent me on my way. I was left with the feeling that I would have to join the programme as an act of faith, and find out what it was like by experience.

A few days later the notes arrived, and these made it clear that it was possible for someone recently promoted to make his own job his project (in February of that year I had taken on the job of divisional manager, with responsibility for the two other departments of the division, while carrying on managing my own department). My boss confirmed that I would be on an 'own-job' project — that way he would only lose me about one day a week. So I joined the programme because of moral pressures, rather than the conviction that it would be good for me. My boss had said he wanted me on it and it would have looked feeble or churlish to refuse to try.

Before the first residential period began, we met our project advisers and our project set colleagues.

David Casey called to see me at the factory and we started with an hour's discussion with my managing director, who listed straightaway a number of problems he thought I had; such as my relations with the sales department, my engineers and the hourly-paid. He saw the problems as largely associated with my character, and wanted the programme to fix them. Shortage of time prevented much discussion, and we left for a quick Cook's tour of my patch.

We walked through the departments and met one or two of my key helpers. On a playback much later on, I was impressed by the way the consultant's eye had picked up an important antagonism.

The project set meets for the first time

My colleagues turned out to be a varied, interesting and impressive bunch. There was John Newman, a super-salesman who would later give us some lectures on selling techniques. From the Post Office we had Jim Cowie, a computer training expert and sometime professor of an American military college, who could verbalize his thoughts faster than some of us could think. And sometimes the thoughts were beyond

IT DIDN'T WORK FOR ME 51

our comprehension. Bill Prince, a works director from West Bromwich, was another with a gift for putting thoughts into words. Colin Gaskell from St Albans was brilliant, but could not talk fast enough to keep up with his thoughts and stumbled sometimes. We were to encourage him to slow down later. Jim Bond, whose responsibilities were most like my own in turnover and number of helpers, was promoted and dropped out of the programme before the residential course.

David Casey, our project adviser from ALP, with vast experience of management development, began his job of getting us to work properly as a group. He was to find us a refractory lot. Glyn Trollope joined us later as GEC project adviser for our set.

Some reactions to the first residential period

The early part of the course encouraged familiarization of participants and advisers with each other. We worked in project sets discussing each other's projects and problems. We also played a business game and were divided into different groupings to meet other members of the community. There were yet other groupings for particular discussions and, of course, there was the bar.

We could observe distinct changes and adjustments as time went by. During the first week, there was much posturing, smoking of large cigars and the like. This nervous smoking was not repeated in the second week.

At the plenary sessions, some members spoke too much. We analysed the contributions into categories: useful, flippant, verbose or bull. At one plenary, two advisers overexposed their erudition with long descriptions, using a vocabulary to which we were not all yet accustomed. We managed to get discreet messages to all these verbose people. They accepted them with good humour, as their subsequent allusions to the matter showed. However, there was probably lasting damage to some of our inferiority complexes, and plenary sessions fell into disrepute.

At intervals Reg Revans gave us talks on a variety of management topics which were interesting and useful. I particularly remember a graphic illustration of the importance of good communications, and it occurred to me that we were fortunate in my firm in having a management structure that helped good communication down in the workplace. All Reg's inputs were scattered with relevant biblical quotations. Later in the programme, Colin Gaskell was to hear it rumoured that Reg had actually written the Bible.

The business game gave us useful experience in dividing responsibilities among a team and in quick decision-making. It taught us something about the use of capital and such things as cash flow compared with profit. The debrief afterwards, when Tony Eccles and Doug Wood told us how we might have done it, was excellent. Another simulation was designed to help us understand how a project set assists and encourages a participant on an exchange project. It sounds unbelievably complicated at first (it did to us) so, if in doubt, skip three paragraphs.

We were divided into two groups, each with a chosen participant (delegate) who would go on an exchange project with the other group. When our delegate was with us, we would act as a project set, helping him with his project (the other group's problem). When the delegates were exchanged, we would act as the host company with a problem that the visiting delegate would help us to solve (as his project). And vice versa! The incestuous complexity increases further when you hear the project problems. Our problem was the organization of project workshops, the monthly meetings of all participants. Their problem was the measurement of the progress of a project. You followed that?

Each group also had three observers, each with a unique role: one accompanied the delegate to the other group and would report to us how our man had performed. One would observe us acting as a project set and playback to us how we did. The third would observe us acting as a host company and report back.

The delegates were exchanged twice with our problem investigated twice by them, and us interesting ourselves in their problem twice. And vice versa! The observers reported back at intervals. You're still following, I hope? The last straw came when our advisers wanted to comment on the whole performance and make observations about the observers. We groaned. Jean Lawrence felt that cooking the cabbage three times was enough.

One of the elegant cynics among my colleagues thought it was too much playing with words. My opinion was stronger.

Another colleague thought we were all being taken for a ride with action learning, a case of the emperor's new clothes. Our super-salesman was worried about the expensive waste of our time (five pence a minute, five pence a minute — each). My contribution to cynicism was the super-redundancy scheme. The theory of this scheme was as follows. During the nine months, our bosses would discover whether our deputies could hold the fort in our absence. At any time they could get us back, but if they found they could spare us at the end, there would be a saving per annum thereafter that was a 100 per cent return on the cost of the course.

It was in this first residential period that we had the first of several black Tuesdays. Many of us got angry that our time was being wasted by not having sufficiently specific or demanding tasks. Then we stayed at DISC for the second weekend (to prove we could work?) and our time was again largely wasted. We could have been at home with our families.

The project set working

Our project set met once a week at first. We visited each of our factories in turn and had a Cook's tour at some time during the day. Some of my colleagues thought these tours were a waste of time, but I am always interested to see other people's facilities and engineering. At my factory, the set members had a chance to meet the directors and other managers, and this helped to identify them when I spoke later of my work in the set meetings.

In the project set meetings we listened to descriptions of each other's projects and progress, and joined in with discussion and advice. It was my impression that none of us, including myself, took much notice of advice given. We will never know if the projects went any differently as a result of our discussion.

At one point our project adviser suggested an experiment where a particular colleague sat silent and listened while the rest of us described what we thought he did well, what he did less well and what points he might improve. With hindsight, this episode was probably hurtful and unhelpful to the individual concerned.

Special training and advice

Training in the skills necessary for the investigation and implementation stages of our projects was given at both residential phases. In October we concentrated on investigation skills and in February on implementation skills.

Participants also asked for lectures on a variety of specialized subjects such as accountancy and project management. These were arranged for February and were much appreciated.

We were also pleased to have the chance to hear from a variety of eminences from the world of business, politics and journalism. They each gave us their ideas on Great Britain's troubles and what we should do to climb out of them.

During the programme, it had become clear to the GEC project advisers that managers at our level suffered from a number of misapprehensions about how GEC worked. In order to give us the authorized version, they arranged for senior GEC managers to come to talk with us in groups about how they and the company worked. We would be better prepared, as a result, to ask better informed questions of Sir Arnold when he came.

Near the end of the February residential period, Sir Arnold came up for an evening with us. The first two hours were given over to a question and answer session with AW alone with the participants and Mike Bett. More of our misapprehensions were put to bed as we listened to the man himself. At the same time, he got a feel of some of the half-truths that get about. We were impressed by his brilliance and could understand why he had the top job. He entertained us with some delicious opinions that could not be published. We asked some fairly cheeky questions and got good frank answers. Altogether a memorable evening.

Disillusionment sets in

But after his visit further set and workshop meetings seemed an anticlimax. People began to be tired and bored. We agreed to reduce the number and length of meetings towards the end.

It was clear that the ways in which my set could help me with my problems were limited. In any case some of the problems had eased or gone away, or may never have existed at all. I had to deal immediately with day-to-day problems at work. I could not save them to discuss with the set first.

Completing the programme was now just a test of stamina. It was time-consuming and travelling was expensive, but to give up would indicate a lack of moral fibre. For a while there were no jobs for a number of the exchange participants. Their old jobs had been filled behind them and there did not seem to be new jobs for them to go to. The jibe about the super redundancy scheme began to look deadly serious. But they would all find jobs, as time would show.

I was openly cynical, but there were others who kept quiet about it. One participant did not want to criticize the course for fear of reducing the value of the qualifications of having been on it. That is cynicism squared.

Final efforts to find benefits for me

It occurred to me that it might be an advantage to have some of my shortcomings mirrored by these set colleagues, well away from my place of work. I asked them to give me the treatment we had given another colleague earlier and which I felt at the time had not been useful to him.

In the event, I felt they were pulling their punches. They were a bit too kind, even flattering in places. The serious criticisms I was expecting. I had already noticed the faults and stubbornly refused to correct them — they were too much a part of me. I thanked them for their help nevertheless.

My managing director had asked several times to see a project set at work, so we invited him up for the day on one of our last meetings. We dealt first with progress on two of the exchange projects and then they got round to my problems. My colleagues stirred it for me by pointing out where my problems were aggravated by actions of my managing director and others at work. I got quite warm, but I need not have worried. My boss didn't notice and commented later that 'Now you know how to deal with your problems'.

Benefits versus costs of the programme

Head office discovered many misapprehensions among managers just below Sir Arnold Weinstock's horizon. He sees our bosses at least once a year at budget meetings — our level, never. We were particularly concerned that the reporting system had influences for the worse on such things as capital investment and research and development expenditure. We had formed common interest groups to refine these ideas and we were fairly certain that some of the messages got back to head office and they tried to do something about it. Our meetings were probably a source of intelligence on all sorts of matters. GEC announced that management training was respectable and set some ideas moving on the subject.

I believe the exchangers got considerable training benefits from being challenged to do a different management task for about eight months with fewer of the normal hazards — a bit like practising in an aircraft simulator. Participants on 'own-job' projects like myself benefited as did exchangers from hearing all the expert opinions at the many meetings. We probably got little use from discussing our own jobs. However, we were only away from our jobs 25 per cent of the time and we made some of this up by weekend and evening work.

But the cost of the programme in extra expenses, time and discomfort, particularly for exchangers away from home, was huge. There would need to be some very special benefit to warrant this expenditure on a regular basis. If the training is to be effective, nominators, participants and clients must all be convinced of the value of such a programme. Arm twisting to produce participants or projects does not give the faith or commitment necessary to obtain maximum benefit from the experience. Participants must not be sent on the programme because they are spare. Remedial work is much better done at home base. Preparation must start early and be thorough. In the circumstances ours was late and sketchy.

Participants should be given projects that are major business problems — simple problems involving tedious clerical work will not train future senior managers. They must also be important problems for the clients, so that they are determined to get them fixed. Exchangers should be told that there will be new jobs at the end of the programme, and these should be arranged as early as possible. They should not be distracted from their projects by worries about whether their company wants them or not.

Reconsidered feelings on management development

Looking back over my work in industry, it is clear that job changes have given the best learning opportunities. It is self-evident that there are then new things to learn, but there are also opportunities to test one's experiences and conclusions in a new situation and adjust or discard ideas as necessary. Such learning should be accompanied perhaps by brief training courses in specialized subjects.

In this action learning programme some participants were encouraged to use their new jobs as projects. The special projects culled from a man's own job were also a form of job change, just as an exchange was.

Bosses must learn to give feedback and guidance kindly and regularly, but especially during the learning period after a job change. Before recent legislation made it less likely, it was too often the case that staff first heard of a complaint against them when they got the sack or were demoted. Groups of people discussing similar work or working on a project together might break down some of the barriers to frankness, but it all costs.

The first GEC action learning programme seemed very expensive for the training benefits obtained. But GEC learned a lot about itself, and perhaps should continue these programmes at intervals and on a smaller scale, to obtain these other benefits.

For myself, I look back on the first programme with mitigated pleasure. As with any uncomfortable experience, the humorous side of it can be seen in retrospect — it reminded me of a first class hike in pouring rain, or a rough Channel crossing — turbulent but interesting.

8
Now . . . to run a company

A project within his own company, but outside his own job, by a GEC manager

COLIN GASKELL

> Dr Colin Gaskell is currently in his second term with GEC, as technical manager of Marconi Instruments. Previously he 'action learned' his way round two universities and three other companies. Dr Gaskell is a chartered electrical engineer.

There is a general view in business that management, like sex, is an activity which gentlemen engage in, but do not talk about. In many respects DSMP 1 could be considered as an orgy of management discussion and like most orgies it tends to leave the participants exhausted, with no clear image of any very particular part of the proceedings. However, six months down the line, the mist is starting to clear and some positive areas of new knowledge are being revealed.

Interesting learning

The first of these is the far better understanding I now have about how GEC operates as a company, in the way that it motivates its senior managers, in the objectives of its chief executive and in the way that the businesses within GEC operate and the scope and limits of the authority of the men who run these businesses. It may seem strange that it should need a programme such as this for an executive to understand something about the company for which he works. But in an organization like GEC, where the devolution of autonomy to the local managing director is almost complete, opportunities for the exposure of even quite senior executives to any level of corporate decision-making and strategy are strictly limited. It would, however, seem desirable to make this kind of contact with top management available to a much wider range of managers than could ever be covered by programmes of the DSMP type.

Before embarking on the programme I read that action learning was really intended to teach one something about oneself. Increased self-knowledge is a difficult thing to analyse in retrospect, but the thing which struck me most forcibly was that the general approach to problems in a significant number of the GEC managing directors that I have met in the programme seemed to be very similar to my own. Whether this should be regarded as an encouraging sign for me, or a terrible warning for GEC, only time will tell.

I have found, like most others, that involvement in this programme was unsettling, particularly in that my career expectations have been considerably raised. When I embarked on the programme the job I now hold was as far up the ladder as my ambition ran. I now have the clear objective of running a business at some point in the not too distant future, hopefully within GEC. For this reason it may be that management development programmes of this kind could show more obvious signs of success in organizations which have a greater degree of career planning than is practicable within the decentralized organization of GEC.

Stay-at-home projects are difficult

As far as the outside world was concerned, and to an extent as far as participants were concerned, the most visible part of the whole programme was the project. In this respect, my position was slightly unusual because I remained in my own job, but took a project within my own company that was not at that time a direct part of my job. The project was concerned with the method of defining a particular aspect of corporate policy for my company. I think that it was generally agreed by myself and my client, who was the managing director, and possibly by the rest of my project set (although they have been too polite to say so), that my project was not brought to a successful conclusion. In part, this was due to the fact that this particular problem — like many which are dealt with by senior management — was not amenable to a simple, neat, logical solution within a short time frame.

Other projects, particularly those concerned with various kinds of information gathering, did appear to have neat solutions, but the real learning value of such projects must be open to some question.

A second difficulty, common to those participants who stayed within their own companies, was that I was possibly too close to this particular problem to take a completely objective view. Although it was not strictly a part of my job, I had been in the company long enough to have formed some views on the subject and it might have been easier for a complete outsider to be more objective. Again, my situation is somewhat unusual in that towards the end of the programme my job function was changed in a way which now gives me a greater responsibility for just that particular area of corporate policy where the project lay. It is now becoming clear that there may be a solution, but it is messy, complex and will take years to implement and test.

This difficulty of maintaining any degree of objectivity about the project was perhaps compounded by a particular worry which the project set encountered in its early meetings. These were dominated by discussion of one participant and his project, where the difficulties were severe. For this reason the investigation phases of all the other projects were carried out with the minimum involvement of the rest of the set. Thus the pattern of each project was formed by the individual almost without reference to the set. This made it very difficult to use the set as a resource in the later stages. It was, perhaps, the lack of assistance with my project from the set meetings which was the most disappointing part of the programme.

The difficulty encountered in the early meetings was not the only reason for this lack of help. Another factor may have been me. Perhaps my own personality made it difficult for me to accept help from the group and the presentation style of procedure which was adopted by the set. This style tended to produce an essentially one-way flow of information and therefore limit the amount of help that the rest of the set were able to give. It may well be that this is normal group behaviour for managers with substantial decision-taking experience, which would tend to militate against either accepting assistance from others in the decision-taking process, or criticizing decisions taken by others. Certainly, the set's discussions of wider management topics were of much greater value and helped me to clarify my ideas on a range of issues of vital concern to most managers in industry. Even the early barrier to smooth set working, referred to above, yielded some valuable insight into the problems of utilizing a certain kind of personality in a senior management position and also the difficulty in formulating a helpful approach to this particular kind of personality.

How have I changed?

I still find it very difficult to assess the changes which have occurred in my own personality and general attitude to management. Identifying the change was much more difficult for those of us who stayed in our own companies, especially those who stayed in their own jobs. For one thing the benefits of the programme seem strangely hidden from one's normal colleagues. If one can judge by their reactions, it would seem that the whole exercise was a waste of time. Their attitude to the programme was dubious at first and became increasingly hostile as the time elapsed. This was in part due to the increasing work load they would have liked me to carry in my job, but in recent discussions they have made it clear that they could not see that either I or the company had obtained any great benefit from it. Perhaps their view is based on the difficulty of seeing incremental change at close range. If this is so it is a significant factor to be considered in later programmes which may include own-job options, because it seems a pity that, when one has learned so much, so little of it is visible in the short term to close colleagues.

9

Communication is the key to getting commitment

A technical manager takes on a systems problem in another part of GEC

BARRY SCOTT

> Barry Scott is a production manager with GEC Marconi Ltd, having previously been engaged in design and development management for five years. Mr Scott is a member of the Institution of Electronic and Radio Engineers.

The initial attraction of the programme was the opportunity to examine another business from an offline position. It would allow me to assess my own management judgement against other managers actually in action. I had already concluded that organizations can busy themselves with inadequately challenged or illconceived objectives. So I had anticipated that eventually some interesting involvement in basic policy examination would occur, regardless of the nature of the project brief. Also, the prospect of managing myself in a totally unfamiliar situation with little or no relevant experience seemed to present considerable opportunity for personal development. A daunting prospect!

Beginning the project

During the introductory visit to the works director it emerged that the works were having considerable difficulty in coping with the large product range and the modifications demanded by the customer, or caused by engineering errors. To aggravate the situation further the customer's specification was liable to be changed right up until final packing was in progress. The solution as perceived by management was to move towards greater standardization of products supported by a standardized documentation system. It was thought this would reduce the blockages in production. This policy was based on a conviction that the market would find the resultant improvement in price and delivery more significant than the ability to demand modifications to the product. This strategy seemed reasonable and was reminiscent of my experience as a technical manager. I had often found myself in conflict with the sales department, which seemed to take orders regularly for products with specifications that differed from the original design.

Having apparently developed a framework of understanding and general agreement, the works director and I proceeded to my first meeting with the managing director. The managing director emphasized among other things the importance of the levels of stocks and work in progress, and the need to increase output per person. Also, product changes were clearly prominent in his thinking. The intended relationship between the three of us was talked about. It was agreed that, while the managing director was the client, I would deal with the works director.

After the visit I reflected that a reduction in stock and work in progress, increased output per person and a standardization philosophy all seemed complementary. So my initial perception of a marketing bias in the project receded.

At my next meeting with the works director, he referred to the mass of problems which seemed to be a permanent feature of the works. After this second meeting it was very clear that a serious problem or set of problems existed somewhere, and the effects were being experienced largely in the works areas. By this time I had decided that I would investigate the company and try to relate product changes to stocks and work in progress, in order to develop a clear policy on standardization.

After quite a lot of difficulty in trying to plan an unknown entity, I decided that my use of time during the project should be:

1	What is the business?	2 weeks
2	How is it performing?	4 weeks
3	How could its performance be improved?	4 weeks
4	What are the objectives?	2 weeks

5   What should be done to achieve
    this improvement?   2 weeks
6   Implementation of recommendation.   12 weeks

I concluded that too much planning could lead to a closed mentality and chose the relative discomfort of continuous reassessment. This approach was approved by the managing director during a brief discussion shortly before the investigation phase commenced.

Entry into the company

I decided to find out what was happening in the company as opposed to what was intended to happen. I reasoned that this called for concentration on nonmanagerial personnel, leaving further discussions with senior management until I had gained firsthand knowledge of the operation. Consequently, my entry into the company was brief and unheralded. The first interview with sales staff of the 'front end' actually started midmorning on the first day. On reflection this initial approach and its subsequent continuation was probably the principal factor which militated against my achieving effective change in the company. I did not establish the correct ongoing communication with management, which is the seat of power.

One important principle of learning which occurred to me early on in the programme was that personal learning followed personal experience at an interval of time which somehow related to the individual.

In four weeks I conducted approximately 30 interviews as I moved from the sales department, through contracts and into the applications engineering department. Throughout the interviews I concentrated on product change, querying the source and degree of change in order to establish a general picture. I concluded that, for the product group under investigation, approximately 80 per cent of production was standard, 15 per cent was standardized (options), and the remaining 5 per cent comprised customer specials. I also gained a clearer impression of the company organization. Several product groups were arranged according to market sector, each group placing its requirements on one of two geographically separate production units.

I became submerged with data and had to concentrate hard on whether there were any patterns hidden behind the endless information streams. I found such permanent concentration very demanding and recognized the difference between this new activity and a job with established routines. I also realized that in general I received answers only to the questions I constructed. I became more aware of the possibility that fundamental issues could be escaping detection.

At the end of the first month I concluded that the commercial and design departments of the business, at least for that particular product group, seemed free of any fundamental error. I had also concluded that it was vital for the customer to be able to demand modifications to the standard design.

I was now in a mildly apprehensive state since I had not established, even in my own mind, any particular avenue for improving the business. I also realized that being one's own boss, free from system constraints and monitoring routines, produced enormous motivation to sustain personal effort. The course of events was entirely the result of my own actions. I worked long hours, preoccupied with questioning my understanding of the situation and the direction of further action.

Entry into the works

I started my investigation of the works with a clearer understanding of management's perception of the problem and the general solution. Apparently, the company saw the causes for their production problems in customer specifications which differed from standard, subsequent customer changes, engineering design errors and changes, and the unreliability of some suppliers. The solution was seen in standardized products and documentation procedures. It was felt that this would:

1 Achieve customer acceptance of standard products, through the incentives of reduced cost and shortened delivery.
2 Minimize new design work, and so bring about a corresponding reduction in the risk of errors.
3 Enable a basic stock policy to be implemented, alleviating dependence on suppliers.

The works management endorsed the standardization policy, but stressed the problems of late information from commercial areas which caused considerable problems in meeting timescales. My next step was to examine the documentation system and problems associated with changes. I spent several days tracing the various channels and for a time became immersed in the computerized stock control system.

Still not aware of any fundamental discrepancies in the works documentation, I returned to question the controllers about the source and effect of changes. Patiently my questions were answered until a senior controller stated that changes didn't cause him too much trouble, but lateness of locally manufactured items did. The lateness of internal supplies cropped up again on another occasion. I associated it with the production manager's comments about late information from commercial areas and wondered what lateness really implied. Further investigation revealed queues in many works areas. While I was still trying to assess the effect of changes and relate such issues to a standardization policy, I selected what was said to be the main holdup area and queried the cause of lateness. It soon became evident that considerable overloads occurred in the department as a whole and on the individual resources within it. The way in which a single machine became overcommitted was identical with what happened to a department and to the whole works unit. The lateness of information from commercial areas could also be associated with overloaded capacity.

I discussed my findings and tentative conclusions with the works director and described with a few diagrams how queues were building up at random within the works (and possibly within the whole business). The response seemed favourable as, within the hour, I found myself in front of the managing director, somewhat unprepared for a second presentation. This time I described the state of the works in terms of 'queuing theory' and suggested that a 'transfer function' could be evolved for the works (and perhaps the whole business) to establish in advance the effect of a change in the mix of products sold. Such a model would allow prediction of resource requirements in advance and thus avoid overall delays on delivery and work in progress.

The management of change appears to be particularly relevant to organizations engaged on low-volume manufacture of a wide variety of specialist products or systems. The effect of mix and specification changes on cost, delivery and investment can be significant, if resource requirements are not recognized sufficiently early. In such situations, organizations instinctively evolve systems designed to aid management control and organizational stability. Medium-term vision seems essential if potential problems are to be recognized and appropriate action taken. Unfortunately, as the rate of change approaches the response time of the system, a relatively useless report on what is happening is often produced as opposed to an indication of what may happen.

In this situation the natural reaction of the administrator is to strengthen the system, either directly with the appointment of new people, or indirectly by calling for more support from line managers. This, in turn, leaves less energy to cope with the reality of change and a level of permanent crisis sets in concurrently with the Parkinsonian growth of administration. I have found that by allocating personal responsibility and establishing freedom of action, people will respond and cope with change much more effectively than a system will.

The managing director listened attentively and queried whether I had outlined such conclusions to the works management in general. Several days later, having discussed the issue with various members of the works, I became very aware that my credibility as a source of assistance to the company had been considerably diminished. Apparently, both the nature of my observations and the manner I had used to describe them had created an image of academic detachment.

I learned that one essential characteristic of an effective manager is the ability to use simple ideas and simple words to describe a complicated situation. Such simplicity is essential if effective communication and commitment is to be achieved between managers in different disciplines with different perceptions of a given situation. If the words one selects are even slightly ambiguous, understanding and commitment in others are unlikely to be achieved.

I produced an interim report which described how various resource areas were being severely overcommitted, causing interruptions to production and adversely affecting the return on investment. It suggested that, while the general standardization philosophy had merit, the market characteristics demanded a level of change to which the organization was not designed to respond.

The report produced little reaction, which convinced me that the way I was communicating with the directors, and the subject matter of those communications, were no longer effective. The error of not gaining a personal commitment from those with authority in the organization became very clear. I set out to redress the situation.

At the next meeting I described the positive correlation between the overdue order book and those products which made demands on the greatest number of resources. I suggested that the superior performance of the first product group which I had investigated was strongly associated with its dependence on the least number of common resources. That presentation seemed to generate interest, but little commitment.

My confidence in my ability to analyse and communicate was beginning to waver. I realized that if I, with every opportunity, failed to communicate a serious operational problem to management, what chance did the lower echelons have? This problem of upward communication within organizations became very apparent.

I now see much more clearly how downward communication in organizations is easily realized while upward communication based on reason is generally much less effectively achieved. In consequence, it becomes apparent that the organization will do tomorrow that which it did yesterday unless change is instigated. Most significant changes are still instigated by senior management as a result of the various streams of information which flow through the management channels. Unfortunately, operators and lower levels of supervision seem to share a very weak upward information stream, probably due to their inability to describe their problems or ideas in a way which gains commitment. Consequently the relevance of this upward stream to management may progressively decrease until upward communication becomes nonexistent. The management response to operational problems, with the information available to them, may well be to instigate policies which will not solve the actual problems of the organization.

As a result of this piece of learning I was determined to try and correct this particular deficiency when I got my new job after the completion of the programme. So, with this conviction in mind I recently arranged for the shopfloor of my new production unit to discuss in groups of eight those issues which they believed limited productivity. Significant factors were listed and returned for my attention. These returns not only showed that serious problems existed but also revealed — once again — that the conventional line management hierarchy was ineffective as a shopfloor-management communication channel. Subsequent management action has been accompanied by a marked rise in productivity. It is particularly interesting to consider that such group meetings enabled the shopfloor to communicate with itself more effectively.

Personal overload

During the early stages of the programme, and totally outside the scope of my project, I had criticized the understanding of 'people at work' as a whole. I had suggested that the present financial reporting systems between Stanhope Gate and the operating companies did not effectively measure the state of human assets within the operating companies. I was asked by Stanhope Gate to explain these convictions, and to make practical proposals for change. These were even more fundamental problems to explore.

Creative thinking became progressively more difficult, essentially because of the overwhelming conviction that I hadn't really achieved anything, and this despite a level of personal effort higher than at any time in my working career. I also recognized the utter worthlessness of words, writings and ideas which, for various reasons, simply do not inspire action.

Eventually I reasoned that if I was anything of a manager, I would step back and reassess the situation I was in and what I was trying to achieve, an ability which I thought I had already mastered. I lowered my sights and resorted to creating a small change in the works as opposed to a large change over the company. To this end I concentrated on working with a small group of middle managers who had recognized their problems. Over several weeks we made some changes in the way their particular resource areas were managed.

The time is up

There remained approximately six weeks before the project formally ended. Senior management was now convinced that resource management was largely a matter of getting the general production flow under control. It was my opinion that the business we were dealing with was anything but a flowline business, despite the attempts to make it so by a policy of standardization. The particular levels of production were the critical factors in my view. I did some further investigation in another GEC company which was sufficient to convince me.

During the remaining weeks I produced a couple of reports on resource management and did my best to find some answers to particular problems of machine-shop loading. Finally, I had dinner with the managing director and his newly appointed general manager. For the first time I established adequate communication. During the evening's discussion, I suggested that my performance warranted four out of five for personal learning but only two out of five for helping his company. His reply suggested that more had been achieved than perhaps I realized.

Action learning and the project set

Throughout the programme I experienced a valuable period of real learning which was often very uncomfortable. There were times when I doubted the efficiency of the experience. I now believe that any real situation has within it the opportunity for learning. There is no doubt that the greatest benefit was in terms of personal communication. My approach to gaining commitment has been substantially revised. Such a fundamental change in personal behaviour would probably only have occurred, if at all, over several years of conventional practice. Our day-to-day environment is programmed to cater for personal deficiencies.

The project set quickly established a high degree of group cohesion. Within this framework of support a high level of personal integrity developed which I have never known to exist in any ordinary industrial situation. One can only speculate on what would be the performance of any business which attained such supportive integrity throughout its organization. In the project set meetings support was counterbalanced by criticism. Initially, such criticism seemed irrelevant. Eventually, however, the persistent pressure of the set was effective in creating a definite awareness of personal shortcomings in mannerisms and style.

The highspot was the degree and quality of debate which usually existed at our meetings. Such debate satisfied the vacuum produced by years of working to a routine which does not cater for such needs.

While the set provided support for its members, the advice on operational problems was usually difficult to adopt. It reinforced my opinion that management style is very personal and difficult to alter. But one's performance can be improved by a regular self-assessment aided by others.

The only aspect which may have limited the experience was the need to achieve action by persuasion rather than by authority. Time may reveal that this made the experience all the more beneficial. Achieving results by involvement and consent is still a relatively novel way of getting things done in our present industrial scene.

Part Three
ALP International and Dunchurch Industrial Staff College

10
The challenge was worth it
What the industrial staff college which housed the programme felt

RAY GODSALL

> Dunchurch Industrial Staff College was the spiritual home of the programme. The residential courses and many set meetings were held there. The administration was fuss-free and efficient, and the staff keen.
> Ray Godsall runs DISC as an independent business for GEC. He has been concerned with learning by experience since 1965. For some years he applied simulation learning techniques in the programmes of the business schools at Cranfield, Bradford, Birmingham and Fontainebleau. His interest in action learning centres on applying the concept to the organization rather than the individual.

Dunchurch had two main roles to play in GEC's programme — one in its management and the other in providing an administrative and home focus point. Each role offered its own variety of stimulus. For the first it was one of an intellectual nature and for the second mostly organizational. Each provided quite different experiences and learning.

The opportunity

Conceptual rigor mortis is probably the greatest threat to the continued usefulness of a busy training or development specialist. For most of us, regular opportunities for mental keepfit are limited to the gymnastics of symposia or the reading of radical articles and books. Both media are used only sporadically and are in any case comfortable.

Any challenge they present to personal attitude or concepts is limited in duration and may be switched off or rationalized away in privacy. It is a rare opportunity that forces the need to challenge continuously and reappraise one's ideas and methods for a whole year. This was the opportunity given to Dunchurch in working so closely with Professor Revans and his ALP associates.

Having used the word opportunity, it is salutary to reflect now that, given free choice, probably neither Dunchurch nor ALP would have chosen to share the design and management of this important UK first. Both organizations separately had accepted long ago the principles and tenets of action learning and developed their own approaches to these. With some professional arrogance and selfishness, each may have seen itself as totally competent to manage successfully GEC's remit without help from the other. GEC required otherwise, and both organizations were wise enough to see the importance of the project as greater than the possible constraints of sharing. This supports a tenet of action learning — valuable learning often derives from living with the inescapable!

But oh the agony!

While there was always total concord between ALP and Dunchurch over the fundamental tenets of action learning, there was often debate on the sanctity of these. Challenge and counterchallenge were the order of the day:

'Learning from experience can be both useful and dysfunctional. *We* must ensure that it is useful.'	'Who are we to judge what is useful?'
'To help them learn from their experience more easily and use it, let us give them interpretative tools and skills *we know* they are going to need.'	'When *they* discover that *they* cannot interpret or apply something *they* will ask for the tool they need.'
'They do not know what tools exist or how to ask for them. *We* must at least show them the toolkit.'	'Man is analytical and creative — need will help *them* innovate.'

'They have themselves shaped this element of the programme. *We know* it will not take them to the learning they seek from it. *We* must intervene.'

'Discovering that their structure and vehicle failed will lead *them* to other learning.'

Throughout, the debate seemed to centre on the degree to which the purity of learning from discovery could be interfered with before real commitment to the learning offered was lost. Such debate is healthy and should be expected, but it must be concluded before a programme gets under way. Otherwise management of the learning activity must suffer impairment.

Dunchurch was left reflecting on the morality of expediency. We firmly believe that some purity of method can be traded off with advantage, saving time which can be used for additional learning. Or do we really believe this? ALP apparently believes in the total inviolability of action learning's tenets; it acted as a conscience for Dunchurch's own philosophies. Perhaps, for commercial reasons, we have shaped our beliefs to suit time and cost constraints imposed on us by clients. We trust not, for the responsibilities are heavy.

Heavy responsibilities

The typical programme participant was in the age range 28 to 38 — usually the most critical period in the manager's career development and progression. These are normally also the most critical years in his home life, with heavy mortgage, young and growing family and little time available to share the burdens. In short, these are the years of growing responsibility, stress and aspirations. We ask to take 10 per cent of these valuable years and, in this time, disrupt his home life, interrupt his immediate career security and generally add more stress. His faith is that we can speed and enhance his career prospects.

From the sponsor's point of view, we deprive his company for almost a year of recognizably valuable and scarce managerial resources, disrupt his organization and add the burdens of closing the gap left and of later reopening it or finding another. His faith is that we will return to him a greater, more flexible resource than that which was taken.

The responsibility created for us by the sacrifice and faith of participant and company alike are in themselves no different from those accepted by any business school or similar organization offering courses of substantial duration. But the action learning programme is not typical of the courses given by these institutions. This programme does not have a highly structured curriculum offering acquisition of a given range of management knowledge and skills with or without certificate of proven adequacy at the end, or even a confidential report. For this programme only the concepts and loose working mode are outlined to sponsors and participants.

Without a syllabus or even offering a feedback, participant and sponsor alike, in accepting the proposal, are required to place much more than usual trust in those designing and managing the programme. Indeed, for the sponsor the trust has to be greater than for the participant. In such a programme, where his learning is the essence, the participant can protect his own interests — the sponsor has only the programme staff to protect his.

The manager of an action learning programme must never forget the scale and duality of these responsibilities and he must balance them accordingly.

Organization

Important as are the underlying concepts and methods of any programme none will succeed unless the organization is appropriately responsive. Dunchurch was the 'home' of the programme. What this means is that virtually all formal meeting and teaching sessions took place here, as did the majority of informal sessions, whether of participants or administrators. In this role we were required to provide food, accommodation and the full range of backup that one would expect from a well organized residential conference facility. As the administrative centre we needed to provide the clerical backup and liaison function as well as the staffing, managing and teaching elements which were part of the activity.

For all the staff at Dunchurch, the experience was challenging. For an institution which typically revolves around much shorter, more controlled course activities there were very unusual characteristics to the management in this nine-month, very fluid programme.

Managing the invariably variable

In general the administrator will, with reason, attempt to get maximum utilization of all resources planned well in advance, and thus the availability of facilities at short notice can always be a problem. Yet the array of disparities between participants — in terms of location, jobs, seniority, and so on — is a dimension that has to be lived with. A man whose 'project' is his own job, and who has perhaps to react to a strike threat or a need for an urgent overseas trip, is in a quite different position from someone on an exchange project at a local factory when it comes to availability for project set meetings. Delegates with and without effective deputies are another case in point.

In this situation, the compromise solution with regard to timing and location of meetings is often enforced, and until they learn otherwise participants are unlikely to give great regard to the availability of facilities as a constraint.

On the other hand, there is a degree to which action learning participants are encouraged to be 'entrepreneurial' in their attitudes towards the availability of scarce resources. The group will learn just how much can really be achieved if it puts its mind to it and frees itself of some of the less useful organizational constraints; it comes to believe in testing whether stated constraints are real, imaginary or invented; it is encouraged to believe that successful completion of the project is paramount and that hurling oneself against 'the system' is a valuable learning experience. In this situation, it is easy for last-minute bookings and cancellations to become a feature of participants' requirements and for them to work right through booked meals (and find themselves very hungry later!) or decide to cut their losses and go home before the meal has arrived.

Apart from bricks, mortar and meals, the scarce human resources of the institution (luckily a potentially more flexible resource) can suffer from some of the same delegate requirements. Again — at least from the administrative point of view — there is a lot to be said for carefully planned fulltime use of staff, administrative, clerical and tutorial. The climate of urgency of a project set meeting, and the personalities and expectations of industrial highfliers, can often lead to sporadic raids on the system which can be disconcerting if staff are not capable of coping with crisis, or of changing speed, hours and working practices at short notice. The one- or two-day set meetings, in particular, can lead to marked peaks and troughs in administrative workload.

Send three and fourpence, we're going ...

An action learning programme is an attractive — often glamorous — thing to have around, and many of the institution's staff want to be involved with it. Indeed, the special and longterm nature of the programme means that both staff and participants should be encouraged to have a greater sense of involvement and identity with, even ownership of, each other. This is very valuable in picking up signals and feedback and in meeting the needs of both groups. Equally, in the enthusiasm that tends to be created, everyone wants to help and multiple communication or overkill results with the consequent confusion. In the last resort, it is essential that a single staff member be the focal point for all communications, knowing both what the participants need and the organization can deliver. The prick of bureaucracy must not threaten the healthy fizz of information bubbling up.

It tests us

An action learning programme is, then, a rather special kind of learning experience. Delegates are by definition in a very dynamic situation and one which they are themselves impacting on, and changing. Their priorities will be subject to constant and unpredicted change and are seldom likely to be identical to those of the institution. Administration can thus be difficult. On the other hand, the need for the system to be broadly helpful and supportive is very high, even when the programme appears to be encouraging activities designed to bring about its near destruction.

In the more usual course business, delegates are often uncertain and undemanding, and the learning experiences encapsulated and carefully managed: in some ways, we can often get away with a great deal that is less than optimal. It does us no harm, therefore, to test ourselves against the demands placed upon us by being the hosts for an activity such as this programme.

In the last resort, playing host to it helped us to examine our own effectiveness. Participants have to learn what is and what is not possible in a rational, well run organization. If we are *sure* that we are such a thing, well and good: we should do no more than behave according to our existing inclinations, systems and patterns and leave the delegates to learn from dealing with us. Conversely, it is useful to consider the possibility that those who make the demands are entirely rational and that our own methods and attitudes might benefit from a regular testing and analysis.

11
Don't call me teacher
An ALP project adviser's view from his set

BOB GARRATT

> This particular kind of action learning programme centres around project sets, and the role of set adviser is crucial. One ALP set adviser was Bob Garratt, and in this chapter he gives his own account of the progress of his set.
>
> Bob Garratt has worked in architecture and planning, alternative education, and personal and organizational development in the UK, Ireland and France. He helped develop live-project-based education at the Architectural Association School, was visiting Fellow in Management Education, Ulster College, Belfast, and is currently consultant editor (management) for the Architects' Journal and an executive committee member of the Association of Teachers of Management.

We met at Dunchurch on 8 October 1974 at the first meeting of our project set. There were five of us, Bryan Cooper, Don Howell, Barry Scott, Robin Smith and me. We viewed each other with the bitter-sweet emotions felt at the start of doing something interesting, even important, yet we knew we were all moving into new and unexplored territory. Exhilaration at the release from routines of industrial life mixed with fear of uncertainties ahead made us all outwardly cheery and inwardly anxious.

The projects sounded interesting, imprecise and bigger than one man could handle comfortably. Bryan and Robin were to investigate the changes needed to Post Office standards and specifications to improve the exportability of transmission equipment, thereby helping their joint client, GEC Telecommunications Ltd. Barry was swapping from Marconi Communications Systems into GEC Industrial Controls, to evolve discipline around product standardization. Don had an unusual project, swapping from GEC Turbine Generators into a major department of the Civil Service to help them undertake research in the private sector, as part of a larger project aimed at improving the department's own planning process.

Only Bryan was staying within his own company. The others were exchanging their organizations; Robin from a customer organization — the Post Office — into GEC Telecommunications, and Don into a customer organization, a Civil Service department. I was coming from the worlds of architectural design, education, and French and Irish politics, into what I had heard was the hard, masculine world of British engineering. I was frightened and felt vulnerable as I had no appropriate background discipline. The first project set meeting relieved me a great deal as we were all obviously very uncertain, but enthusiastic, and after exchanging the usual introductions and gabbling quick curriculum vitaes, the conversation moved on to a higher intellectual level than I had expected. We dealt for some time with ideas of truth, values and social history.

Barry and Robin immediately identified themselves as crusaders for social change and industrial democracy, with Barry as the optimist and Robin as the pessimist who saw life as a cosmic joke in extremely poor taste. Don kept his powder dry. These three were in their early 30s, as I was. Bryan, some 15 years older, admitted to being disquieted and rather out of his depth with such talk and brought the conversation back to questions of 'What can be done?' He countered the enthusiasm for ideas, with questions on the practicalities of action, and so established himself as the counterweight of the set. That meeting was more bonding for the project set than any of us realized at the time.

We meet the other three sets

A week later we went into the opening residential period for all four sets. There was great tension and friction at this first meeting of the full programme. Most participants were concerned about the behaviour expected of them by top management. They worried about 'correct' dress and 'proper' deference to authority. They refused to enter discussion in what could be construed as 'political' areas, either internal or external.

Our two crusaders fared badly. Barry was determined to use this one chance to effect organizational change in a direction which he thought good, rather than simply ingratiate himself with senior management (which he supposed others would attempt). His outspokenness and relative lack of social influencing skills did not endear him to the majority. Neither did Robin's behaviour. Coming from outside GEC, he was conditioned to expect myopic and blinkered views. He had hoped that meeting this group of potential senior GEC managers would dispel such stereotypes but during those early weeks it was not to be so. Greatly frustrated, he challenged members of other sets to drop their inauthentic 'senior management' postures and concentrate their efforts on understanding themselves and on doing some real work for a change, rather than talking about others doing work for them. This did little to endear him to the rest of the community. He and Barry were effectively isolated from the main group through their open and challenging behaviour and for most of the programme were seen by the majority as opinionated, unduly vocal and illbehaved.

How the set became bonded

David Pearce joined our set as the GEC project adviser, and we worked on bonding the parts into an operational unit which would support us all during the next eight challenging months. The designers of this initial residential period had placed great emphasis on developing social communication and influencing skills very early in the programme, almost excluding at this stage learning about general managerial ideas and language. This had sound reasoning behind it, but the participants were about to start live projects and felt thwarted by not being given the senior executive language to which they aspired. They resented having to deal so long with such 'soft', 'manipulative' and 'time-wasting' activities as identifying, checking and developing social skills.

I stated from the very beginning that I had little time for T-Groups, grope-groups, psycho-drama or sitting in circles staring at our own, or others', navels. I saw communication skills as being essential for projects. I felt that projects were highly political activities, the success of which rested ultimately on the formation of trusting relationships with the clients. I saw self-analysis and development of individuals as a crucial role of the project set, but thought it naïve to assume that this would be recognized by the clients, sponsors, or casual observers. So we had to be *seen* to be concentrating on the organizational effectiveness problems with which we were faced. GEC seemed too results-and-finance orientated to accept self-development alone as a 'successful' conclusion of an action learning project. If personal development was achieved at all, it would be seen more as a bonus in addition to the project solution. Such a statement led to visible signs of relief within the set and they rapidly, and paradoxically, began talking about their responses to, and feelings about, each other. Inevitably this was crudely critical as at this stage there was little understanding of what 'supportive criticism' meant.

Barry was seen by the set as too ruthless in pursuing his ideas and too unaware of the effect he had on others. Don was too canny and low profile and was urged to drop his consultant image and let his emotions show through. Bryan was seen as the 'company man', slow to accept new ideas. Robin was too cynical and abrasive. David was too reticent and was generally reckoned to be a Stanhope Gate spy — although this idea was quickly dispelled when he put his position at risk as much as anyone else, by talking frankly about himself within the set.

I was left pretty much alone, because I was unclassifiable in managerial or professional terms, because I was initially seen by the set (to my annoyance) as a teacher, and because I tried to be anonymous in the set. I rarely said anything on the technical aspects of the project, concentrating on the participants' behaviour and their problem-solving strategies, acting more as a learning catalyst, umpire, and tutor. I literally kept my head down to take notes throughout the programme, feeding these back to the set as a running diary of their personal development on which they could reflect, reorganize their thinking, and eventually modify their behaviour.

Outside attacks on Robin and Barry by the rest of the programme helped bond the set together. Don, too, had expressed strong and vocal opinions which were not universally accepted. Bryan thought a lot of these external attacks unfair and illconceived. So these two increasingly supported the other two. The set saw the other sets as being primarily concerned with conserving the existing organizational and reward systems. We saw management more as a dynamic balance between change for the future and maintenance of the extant.

At this time, we ran into a special problem which neatly dated a point in the history of the set. David Pearce had said from the start that he was only temporary, and that another GEC project adviser (John Shrigley) had been appointed for the set. During the heady days of bonding in the set, David had been present but John had not. When John presented himself towards the end of the second residential week, he was rejected outright. This was not because he was seen as intrinsically bad (the set did not know him) but rather because he had not participated in the initiation rites and could therefore never be one of 'us'. John admits that he was very annoyed by this rejection at the time. He had put great effort into freeing himself for the nine months of the programme. Attending a programme such as this was not usual behaviour for a personnel director within GEC. The 'baron' had to be carefully persuaded that this would be in his group's short and longterm interest. Then to have this effort thrown back in your face without being given the chance of stating your case was really too much. John says that he drove angrily down the motorway. However, he decided against tackling this novel problem by using his status as a personnel director to demand entry to the set. He would do it by persistence and persuasion, through simply being silently there when the set met until he became accepted and was found to be useful. Such persistence and humility paid off within a month and John became a very powerful member of the set, being particularly helpful in giving a GEC viewpoint when the participants discussed their analyses and implementation strategies.

In a mood of euphoria at our compatibility, truculence with the rest of the programme, and trepidation for the future, we entered the projects.

The analytical stage

I will concentrate on what I saw the participants attempting to do in generalized terms, what I thought they should be doing, and how the set tried to develop in all of us a personal methodology for managerial analysis, implementation, testing and learning. In the simple model of action learning the first half of the programme would be analysis and the second implementation. But it did not happen as clearly as that. We rapidly found that as soon as you touched something that had been defined by the client as a problem the damned thing moved, seemed to change colour and shape and split into many other problems. This made analysis of the problem, in the simplistic form as taught in most technological and scientific institutions, almost impossible. There was no baseline from which to measure, and no universally agreed units by which to measure. In the technical systems that we were observing, the people in each organization kept intervening to cloud the measures. The set began to learn slowly and painfully about the difficulties of assessing human systems in organizations. At first, this learning was undertaken reluctantly because it was messy and uncertain, and quite against our previous education. Later there was more enthusiasm, and toward the end of the programme it was given a firmer, philosophic basis when the set could relate it to the hard sciences.

The analogy was drawn between, say, Heisenberg's Uncertainty

Principle, derived from quantum mechanics (that the very act of observing, changes both that which is observed, and the observer) and the soft science ideas on behaviour as seen in, for example, the Hawthorne Effect and Action Learning Theory.

As individual approaches to methodology were developed within the set through mutual criticism, we ran into some basic problems with the development of personal skills and attitudes. There was a reasonable level of numeracy within the set, so the 'number crunching' activities for analysing technical data proved essentially mechanical. However, the level of literacy in the set was a different matter. We had difficulty in reading effectively and rapidly and, therefore, usually opted not to read at all — even newspapers. Writing succinctly was difficult, but as action learning projects did not require a report at the end, this released us from any obligation to put thoughts on paper in a logical manner, or so the argument seemed to go. We had difficulty in talking effectively and precisely and were very bad at listening to what others were saying, as opposed to hearing what we thought others should be saying. I was chastised for making these personal deficiencies explicit (and am to this day). But the initial grudging acceptance of the need to develop effective personal communication skills was transformed into enthusiasm for doing so as the projects became more directly concerned with the people who comprised the organization, including the personal relationship being forged between the participant and his client.

Early bruises

The entry strategies to the analytical stage of three projects showed very different approaches. Barry interpreted his brief as 'putting the organization right' and decided to submerge without trace into the grassroots of Industrial Controls, to get a real feel of the organization before attempting to discuss with the senior management and his client the problems he would find. This interpretation of the brief was regularly challenged by the set but to little avail at this stage.

Bryan and Robin, working together on their project, carried out a series of broadly selected interviews across GEC Telecommunications to chart existing views of the problem area. Their strategy was to map the problems related to specifications as seen by the two opposing sides, GEC Telecommunications and the Post Office, and then help open negotiations on changes, based on a mutual appreciation of these problems.

Don had prepared with the civil servants a very carefully designed study programme against which he and they monitored progress. He was to contribute his information-collecting activities to a rolling debate, which was testing working hypotheses within the department. Don's was the only strategy and performance specification clearly stated.

Barry's approach was heavily criticized within the set. After this, he paid much more attention to some powerful but simple interrogation and project planning procedures that Don had found helpful in his previous consultancy work.

Robin and Bryan had seen such a need earlier and had grudgingly begun to plan and monitor their project methodically, with the set checking at each weekly meeting if they had done what they said they would.

The uncertainties of politics

As the projects progressed through the analysis stage, there were significant increases in the participants' self-confidence, through their increased understanding of the technical aspects. They became more adventurous in analysing the apparently intractable problems on the people side of the organizations. But there was still great fear that opening up such areas would put the participants in too exposed a position in the client company, and make them too visible within the total organization for their personal career safety. Gearing up to face the client organization's politics and the consequent pain of seeing oneself reflected through the eyes of the client and others was a major stage in the development of the projects, of individuals and of the project set. It put a great stress on the GEC project advisers as they had to keep the confidentiality of the set and this at times challenged their loyalty to the larger organization.

Open analysis of the political systems of the organizations cut across the existing rules for good behaviour in GEC managers. The rule was to seek organizational invisibility, since managers were all in competition with each other for career development and the prizes were given to those who conformed most. To attempt to take a detached and rational view of a total organization and make criticisms, not just of the technical systems but of the behaviour involved, was quite against the grain. Such criticisms could be made privately among consenting adults but to make them face-to-face with the people concerned, and some of them chief executives at that, was not only irresponsible but career suicide. It handed your enemies the weapon of your destruction. The received truth was that organizational invisibility ensured survival through the avoidance of risk.

How were such attitudes to be countered? They are damaging in times of continual economic and social turbulence, where the rate of learning within an organization must be equal to or more than the rate of change in the external environment. Within our programme they were challenged and debated through the structure and process of the project set. Reg Revans' description of a set being a 'group of comrades in adversity' had raised sniggers at the start of the programme. Now it became real as the participants were distanced from their home organizations and as increasing hostility was felt from the client organization, where personal and corporate behaviour, rather than technical systems, came under the participants' scrutiny. The set members were thrown back on their own personal qualities and values and had to undertake more self-analysis and debate on personal objectives before being able to articulate the amount of personal risk each was willing to take, and for what end, when analysing the politics of his client organization. Our set had this strong theme of altruism and social change running through it, so the debating was intense and dramatic. But how does one translate this into action, Bryan continually asked us?

The idea of entitlement emerges

We developed the idea of managerial 'entitlement'. Just as a manager has rights and duties which make up the contract between himself and the organization, so a participant has rights and duties between himself and his client organization. In return for the analysis he makes to help the client with the nominated problem, the participant has a right to be listened to and to generate debate within the client organization. But more than this, a participant has a duty to generate within himself an objective for that organization which he feels *entitled* to pursue for the longer term benefits of the people of the organization. Such entitlements were slowly emerging and being made explicit within the set. (Acknowledgement is due to Alistair Mant for helping us with the idea of entitlement.)

Barry was particularly incensed at what he saw as the inhuman use of human beings in organizations. He campaigned for honesty, integrity and visibility of management within organizations — and for some measures other than financial ones by which assessments of corporate managements could be made. Bryan and Robin were seeing that inter-organization and intra-organization communications were appalling, at anything other than ritual levels, and were becoming determined to do what they could to rectify matters. Don was beginning to feel entitled to criticize GEC for its apparent lack of planning compared to the organizations that he was investigating. These entitlements were mutually agreed, almost by osmosis, within the set and changed the frames of reference of the initial, nominated projects.

The rise of personal projects

The initial project was suddenly seen as a small and detailed aspect of a personal project, or second project, to which the participant was likely to be dedicated after the completion of the initial project. The set had formulated personal and deeper beliefs now about organizations and people, and in so doing had put their projects into a perspective where an intervention in the politics of the client organization would be motivated by the desire to move it in a direction seen to be 'good' by each participant. They had broken away from the idea of the project as another job and now saw themselves as individuals with a personally designed role in their host organizations. This very uncomfortable process tested the personal qualities of the set to the limit and produced a group of firm friends who have been strongly supportive well after the end of the programme.

Implementation and organizational change

At the start of the programme, Reg Revans had talked of the need for a *'structure d'accueil'*, or welcoming committee, to be identified by each participant on entry to his client organization. The idea was that such people would help the participant understand quickly what the organization was about, then provide the medium for debate and influence within the organization. Finally, they would become the specific people to take action ensuring implementation of the proposals in cooperation with the participant. Little attention had been paid to such an idea within the set, even though each participant had complained to some degree of the lack of cooperation received from clients and those people expected to provide information within the organization.

Until now the project advisers had not fully appreciated the power of this idea. But now we started to push for the formation of such groups, reminding the participants that they would need to identify people with free energy, people with the motivation to back and develop the participant's ideas and people with the political power to effect change once they thought the ideas good. These three energy sources were unlikely to be found in one person and all three needed to be tapped simultaneously and sensitively by the participant. The set came to see that such people must be identified and brought into the project — an acid test of their new communication skills and political awareness.

Barry now paid much more attention to informing his client who had been redefined as the managing director rather than the works director. He involved him in debate, while developing and implementing through a small and highly motivated group in the Kidsgrove factory, a pilot project which (if suitable) would be transferred to Rugby as the basis of the new production control system.

Robin and Bryan were now operating at an organizational level so much higher than they initially envisaged that at times they would break into a cold sweat. The investigations within GEC Telecommunications had gone well technically, but there seemed little enthusiasm by senior management to do much with the results in the near future. In the Post Office, too, they were faced with low motivation to take action. By bombarding both senior managements with some very well written critical reports, a degree of enthusiasm was sparked, but direct action was blocked by the entrenched negotiating rituals and trials of strength dramas, between the manufacturers and the Post Office, over specifications and orders.

Having got this far, Bryan and Robin saw the need to open channels of communication between the two massive organizations at higher levels. They searched for allies within the two organizations. Whilst verbal support was easy to find privately, public action was very hard to come by. Diligent reading of the relevant Acts and White Papers concerned with the national interest related to nationalized industries, and a study of commercial reports on Post Office and foreign markets, led to some tricky questions being asked by the two participants about GEC commercial policies — especially in export markets. A flurry of stonewalling was met on all sides at this point. This was broken by direct contact with the Post Office director of development, who was impressed by the quality of investigation and the lines of action proposed and moved matters direct to chief executive levels.

None of the projects had an immediately quantifiable 'hard'

outcome, although one year later there are changes in procedures and behaviour amongst senior management in the client organizations. The project set showed that it was possible to promote both personal and organizational development simultaneously through action learning projects. The next problem for GEC is how to handle such motivated and critical people when they return to their home organizations. The learning here is slow and painful, open to heavy questioning and in need of open debate.

Personal reflections

In my project adviser role, it was possible to observe and comment on the culture and procedures of the total company through thinking about those constituent parts with which one came into contact. The intensity of the antagonism between GEC companies was a major surprise to me. The lack of attention to inter-company communications hit home for me when, following a project advisers' meeting (see Appendix II) monitoring the progress of the programme, the GEC project advisers (who were all personnel directors) stayed and chatted together through the night 'because we never have such chances just to talk to each other — we're always crisis-ridden!' One benefit the programme has begun to show is that, at top middle manager level at least, it is now acceptable behaviour to show inter-company cooperation.

I was also surprised by the apparently universally held belief of the participants that only one managerial style was tolerated within GEC. This was known as the 'blood in the gutter' style. My observations showed that this was not true; there were a diversity of managerial styles operating simultaneously, depending on the personalities of the people involved and on the business environment in which they operated. The paradox that I noted was that the high degree of autonomy given to each operating company had led to a centralized body of myths about the totality, 'GEC', which the lack of communications between the companies helped to maintain and even reinforce. Some of these myths were rudely shattered by the arrival of Sir Arnold Weinstock during the second residential period in February 1975. His ebullient and witty style, coupled with his apparent omniscience, shattered the carefully nurtured organizational myths, especially those concerning him. During his private session with 'his men' his ability to relate national and international trends to each company contrasted with the insularity and anti-intellectualism of the managers present and of their managers back home. Sir Arnold's deep investigation of Barry's intensely stated views on the abuse of people in the organization surprised many who had grown up with a different stereotype of their chief executive.

Just what sort of managerial behaviour *is* now going to be rewarded in GEC? Are the old deferential systems being overturned, or is passion and risk-taking an aberration which will be tolerated only very occasionally? I know what I would like to believe — the former. But learning about changes in acceptable behaviour by individuals in decentralized companies is a slow business, evolutionary rather than revolutionary. At least what was seen by the majority of the participants at the start of the programme as the 'ill behaviour' of Barry and Robin is now seen by them and others as an alternative and more open style of managing.

But I too have been motivated through action learning and begin to feel my own 'entitlement'. I have thus developed a personal project — to get much of what is currently considered alternative thinking about our future social, political, and economic environments debated by senior managers. A change in their perspectives could reorganize their thinking about how to develop their businesses. Perhaps Sir Arnold's creative shortcircuiting of the communication flows in GEC, by debating with the participants on this programme, will encourage others to follow suit within their own organizations. The consequent release of energies, applied to considering their future organizational effectiveness, would lead to impressive action and much learning — and the development of a style of managing more appropriate to the challenges of the 1980s.

12
ALP is learning too

A director of ALP International reviews her programme involvement

JEAN LAWRENCE

> It would be a sorry tale if those responsible for an action learning programme did not themselves learn. The GEC programme was a significant event in the young life of Action Learning Projects International. Three ALP directors were deeply involved and one of them wrote this chapter following her experience as a set adviser.
> Jean Lawrence is senior consultant at Manchester Business School and works as a process consultant with the Tavistock Institute. Previously she had been senior consultant with the Anne Shaw Organisation, after Glasgow University and production management at Cadbury Bros.

The concept of a learning institution is fairly new and not altogether accepted. That ALP has learned and is learning is beyond dispute — perhaps that it is an institution can be questioned. Those involved did not set out to build one.

ALP International Ltd, a non profit-making company, is a collection of 11 people actively committed to action learning. The GEC contract was its first large corporate task. For two years work had been done on roles, structures and finance; on our expectations of the nature of the client relationship; on the ownership of problems and the marketing of action learning. This had involved much testing of each other's concepts, experience and competence which had resulted in the development of a high degree of mutual respect and trust within the group.

The group of 10 (the 11th lives abroad) came together through their common interest and a shared need to develop opportunities to work in action learning. But their backgrounds are very diverse. They include nursing, local government research in the social services, management work in business schools and colleges, line management, and the indefinable Reg Revans whose experience spans almost the whole range.

Differing values and expectations of the work of ALP had been exposed and examined. The subsequent experience showed that this thorough work was too shallow until it was tested by action. Perhaps we should have had one of our number, or someone from outside, clearly defined in the role of learning adviser to the group. He could have helped us be bolder in our explorations and ensure that, until opportunities to act presented themselves, we frequently spent long periods of time clearing away this debris of unshared, unfulfilled expectations and bruised values.

As the quantity and variety of our opportunities have increased, each of us has been able to work with different colleagues. It has been possible for us to explore in action each others' styles, competences and values. More of our expectations are being met. The way to deal with our problem was to begin to act!

ALP as a learning institution

If ALP itself learns, the entity must be changing its behaviour. This must be discernibly different from the learning of the individual members. Our joint understanding of the process of action learning has deepened and the designs for our later work all show evidence of change. The members actively involved in the GEC project provided the inputs to this learning process. They were, however, a small minority group.

When this first important contract was signed with GEC, all 10 ALP board members corporately took financial, legal and operational responsibility for the ALP role in the programme. However, only Reg Revans, David Casey and I were active participants in the programme, with Anita Loring handling the publicity and publication matters.

In its early growth, ALP International had resisted all the trappings of an institution — and it still does. Yet in another sense it is an institution, an institution in the mind, and is felt to be so by the 10. And the learning — jointly, institutionally, experienced by the 10 — has been at times painful and slow. Learning about programmes, about design and about mistakes in design has proved more fruitful than learning about the differing styles occurring in project sets and about the roles of the client and of the company project adviser for instance. Writing this some 18 months later, the emphasis has changed and the focus of learning is precisely in these areas.

The first major challenge occurred with the need to accept that some were to be chosen for GEC — and by GEC — and some were not. In the exploration of reasons and criteria for the choices, ALP learned something about the delicate relationship with the client at the beginning of an action learning project — and more about itself. We worked at how far, even at that early stage, it is helpful to the client's learning to persuade, insist, advise, negotiate, stand firm, expose issues, and how far, in given circumstances, these things are possible without jeopardizing the activity to which ALP and its clients are committed. These decisions — how far to push an issue, how much to expose feelings, how much to intervene — were to recur for ALP advisers throughout the programme.

The question remains. Had we persuaded GEC (had we tried even more seriously to persuade GEC) that more learning might result if we involved someone with mainly nursing job experience, but who thoroughly understood the concepts of action learning and was very experienced in the work, is it likely the whole programme would have been abandoned? Or would we have gone ahead but with a less close and confident relationship with the client? How far might that have affected the 'success' of the programme — the level of the participants' learning, the company and company personnel's learning, and the project work achievement?

Perhaps ALP has learned the importance, for future programmes, of helping the main client to accept that it is the provision of learning opportunity that is crucial — not what the adviser 'knows'. Indeed, the adviser's ignorance can often be the touchstone for learning within the group.

Sharing the learning in ALP

Later in the programme our difficulties became more evident. Those of us closely concerned with the GEC programme tried to communicate the experience to our ALP colleagues. They were vitally interested but unable to participate — and, in action, learn. It seemed to be difficult — usually the overt reason was pressure of time — to share very fully the problems, failures, excitements and opportunities in the programme. For me this was a serious failure. ALP International is itself an able and committed set to which to bring one's experiences — joys and difficulties. But, as with all action learning programmes, the passage of time, with committed members working together on understood problems, is essential.

One enormous benefit to be gained from the establishment of an action learning trust might be that there would be pressure to find time for sharing. Perhaps those working full time in action learning, will provide clear opportunities — workshops, seminars, learn-ins — which will encourage others among us to give the requisite priority to working on sharing the experience. It may be that through the action learning trust we may find ways to provide opportunities for others to share in the action in programmes in a way ALP has not yet worked out successfully. A large number of visitors came to the GEC residential phases and were very welcome, but it has not proved easy to involve others in the basic work of the programme for short periods.

There is no doubt that those 'out there' on their own — project advisers and programme coordinators — need the support of others who can share, in the guts as well as in the head, their dilemmas as they happen. ALP is alive to this lost opportunity for learning, and has increased the length of its own monthly meetings to allow a little more time to understand what is being experienced on different programmes. Since all ALP members have fulltime jobs, full-day meetings mean loss of earnings or holiday for some, and an increased backlog of work for others. Again Reg Revans is an exception — he is fully committed to action learning programmes worldwide and has to choose daily which programme he can support.

Shortage of time, so often given as a reason for lack of sharing, is not however the only reason for the difficulty, and it seems important to explore the matter further. Each minority group in ALP concerned with a single programme becomes very committed to that work, and the barrier between those *in* and those *not in* can become higher with time. This phenomenon is seen even more clearly within a programme. The work within the sets was hard and committing, requiring all the energies of set members and project advisers, and loyalty to the set grew quickly. Again we failed to provide enough opportunities for project advisers to learn from each other's experiences in their separate sets.

Sharing the learning inside the GEC programme — the project adviser role

Each adviser managed his own project in the programme; that is, he managed the provision of learning opportunities for the members of his project set. As far as he was able, he helped them recognize the opportunities as they occurred.

The project set is the centre of the programme. The set boundary gradually becomes very strong, with set rivalry developing in many subtle ways. Work is seen as centred in the set. Inter-set activities prove difficult to establish. In the absence of the need for advisers to work across set boundaries, except in the programme management role, there is strong resistance to the association of 'sharing experience' and 'work' or 'learning'. Sharing is regarded as social or, at best, casual in spite of the startling clarity of that association when the words are put down on paper together. Action learning *means* that work, in this sense, and learning are founded in sharing the experiences.

The fact that the work done on sharing learning experience would enhance the performance of the group of project advisers in its management role was missed. At a minimum, the group would be clearer moment by moment just what it was managing. For example, suppose that time is set aside to explore what is happening in each set at one moment in the programme. It might then become clear that three out of the four sets are working, in their very different ways, at issues about the (perhaps perfectly legitimate) withholding of information from lower levels of management and about the misconceptions that result. It may then be worth examining how far this reflects an anxiety about the management of the programme itself. Perhaps there is an underlying anxiety about what information may be held by the management of the programme and what is to be done with it.

'Confidentiality' and 'research' may also feature in the process in the sets and give some clues to what is going on. The managerial behaviour of the project advisers might be changed by this insight — it may, for example, be proposed that space be made in a workshop setting to examine these issues. Or does this phenomenon coincide with the beginning of re-entry anxieties? If this is thought likely to be nearer the underlying reason for the coincidence of three sets being simultaneously concerned with very similar issues, the managerial behaviour might be different.

Little of this work was done in any but the most haphazard way. Issues were picked up over lunch, over the bar, etc., and action was taken. No obvious mistakes were made, but did we miss important opportunities because we did not work jointly on what was there severally in the sets?

Equally, if project advisers are continually to deepen their understanding of their difficult roles and to become themselves more skilled, this sharing is vitally important. It should be built indestructibly into any new design. Otherwise it will be pushed out of the programme in favour of the role in the project sets with its high commitment, excitement, visibility and reward. Habits grow quickly, experimentation may fade in the face of risk to oneself or the possibility of loss to the participants.

All the advisers were experienced in the role in many different circumstances — perhaps in Reed International cadre training, perhaps in Manchester Business School project-based programmes, in live project education in architecture, in joint development activities, or in Tavistock conferences with teachers and social workers.

For the incumbent, however, the adviser role still raises questions all the time. Is it appropriate to interrupt useful work on the project to ensure that attention is given to the hangups of the set member — at this stage in the development of the set? If I leave it they will pick it up later — would that be better? Who, if anyone, should initiate action in this difficult situation between client and participant, especially as the client is the participant's boss? The participant? The adviser? No one? Later? Now? Should the set's apparent belief that nothing should be done, be challenged yet again on the ground that they are in-company men? Confronting the senior man, the boss, may not even yet be acceptable. Or would that only increase their feelings of dependency at this stage in the development of the set? Should I share my feelings of confusion at this point?

And if the participant looks like leaving the programme, should I use that as a learning opportunity for all to explore joint responsibilities, group relationships, boss/subordinate relationships, and the need for individual responsible decision-making? Why am I feeling so confident and able at this moment, though they seem confused and hesitant? How shall I respond to their prodding me to keep him in the programme, for the programme's sake and their image? And if he goes, can they understand and accept my feelings of loss but not of failure, and deal with their own?

Did I miss an opportunity to open up that difficult blocking area, in favour of using the technical knowledge being exposed? If so, why? Why am I feeling so unsure? Am I speaking to protect myself and to build my image, or that they may learn? Am I colluding in avoiding exposing that problem, because of my own need (personal and professional) for acceptance, or am I right that there is not yet sufficient awareness in the group to work on that issue openly and fully? Will there ever be? Or do we have to be satisfied to have worked at the top of the iceberg only?

These are frequent, grinding and gutchurning questions. They are lonely ones in the project set. Sharing with the in-house company project adviser often helped in enabling him to keep on risking himself and taking the consequences. Set members may brutally reject what the adviser is doing but his colleague can provide understanding and support so that he will go on in that direction, though it is painful to him and disturbing to the set members. Only then can the participants feel free to take risks — to expose their difficulties, failures, abilities, expectations and values, and to learn. Their situation in their receiving company may at times be similar, or they may find themselves providing just such support for one of the other set members.

Sharing the responsibility in the programme — the client relationship

Completing the projects and achieving a high standard in project work was not uniformly successful. ALP relearned the lesson that project clients and client groups must be involved and committed from the start. On more recent programmes, various methods of involving clients much more closely at the start are being tried. In DSMP 1 we had a particular problem where participants were working in their own jobs. It was difficult for clients to give high priority to the participant who was simply in his normal work role. Yet that higher level of commitment is required if project work is to be completed successfully.

Renegotiation of the project brief early in the process (and again later if necessary, even many times) is essential to the sharing relationship which must develop. The problem must, from time to time, be consciously recognized as being owned jointly by the participant and by a distinguishable client. Then commitment to a single course of action can be agreed explicitly on each occasion.

Management relationships

There were three paired personal relationships which were crucial to the success of the programme and an institutional triad which was workable and effective. ALP, GEC and DISC worked closely together. Administrative worries were at a minimum throughout the events. The crucial relationships, however, were in pairs — between David Pearce and David Casey; Reg Revans and Sir Arnold Weinstock; David Casey and myself. The first between the two Davids, the GEC programme sponsor and the ALP coordinator, was the cornerstone on which all else rested. At times it seemed unnecessary to distinguish to which of them one was talking and about what, so close was the understanding between them. The approach ALP followed — the early appointment of a project coordinator and the development of a close, one-to-one, relationship with a central GEC manager — was validated on this first project. It is not possible yet to see how far this was a function of the style of the two people concerned, but it certainly was recognized by ALP to be a major factor in the success of the programme.

The relationship between Reg Revans and Sir Arnold Weinstock helped participants, clients, Stanhope Gate management and ALP to focus on the work in the programme. It helped reduce career anxieties. It also encouraged the commitment of resources in the company and outside it to solve problems as they occurred.

The close relationship within ALP between David Casey and myself rested on total sharing of information about the programme events, and joint work on the design. This proved to have been essential when a slipped disc prevented him from leading the last part of the programme. By this time the participants were playing a large part in managing the programme and I was easily able to fill temporarily the role of coordinator.

We recognized the need throughout the programme for a management group which consisted of people from ALP, DISC and GEC. This proved administratively effective and fruitful. Further experience of this kind of action learning programme in the UK will help us to understand better the role and composition of this management, and to experiment with styles of management of programmes.

Sharing Reg Revans

ALP International is a group of equals — but one, Reg Revans, is more equal than the others! In spite of the experience of previous work and of group meetings over more than two years, there may have been a doubt whether ALP would effectively launch and carry through the programme, or whether Reg Revans would. ALP learned by experience that successful programmes can be developed with clients, and that in all circumstances Reg will maintain his own role within the programme, supporting all others in theirs — and that it is neither necessary nor welcome for him to be consulted at every stage.

The deliberate policy of not being profligate in using his skills, but using them at crucial and appropriate times, worked well. He was seen by all to have provided inspiration and kindly personal attention, in spite of international commitments and seemingly endless travel. When he was needed for an event he was there.

Finding resources

Two project advisers were recruited from outside ALP. They and their previous activities were well known to members of ALP. It was not difficult, in one day, for us to generate interest from a dozen known and acceptable names. When approached, all were eager to help, though pressure of work would have prevented a few from making the major commitment required in the adviser role in the programme. So it seems that excellent resources are available for work on action learning programmes. They need not be permanently attached to a body entirely devoted to action learning and perhaps it is better that they are not.

Sharing the achievement

Some learning in the programme was reinforcing: ALP knew it already in some way but relearned it with new insights and perspective. But some learning came as a surprise. For example, the degree to which GEC was changed by the programme exceeded our expectations. The evidence was necessarily small in quantity when one considers the total population, but shifts in attitudes towards participation, and changes in beliefs about communication were consistently reported. The moves towards changing the organization's activities, and not only developing the individual, were apparent in a clear and positive way.

ALP relearned that the work on projects was as important as the management development process going on within the programme. It seems possible that ALP may have colluded in the vogue for manager development and concentrated too much in this area, slightly neglecting to focus on the actual changing of a company's behaviour, embodied in and developing from the work done on the projects, which itself determines that individual learning takes place.

That the participants have learned from their seven-month struggle to plan and carry through a project with a client under the highly critical, if supportive, eyes of four or five colleagues needs no further proof for us.

The client and ALP must both continue to learn

Towards the start of the programme, ALP formulated a policy that, as a company, it would not work with GEC on a second programme, if asked. This was to ensure from the outset that GEC thoroughly learned about action learning and became responsible for it. Also, we wanted to be free to face new challenges and work on new programmes.

Our statement was far more important than was imagined at the time. The certainty, rather than the possibility, of our withdrawal at the end of the programme motivated all GEC managers and advisers to participate fully in every stage and to plan resources for the future. Relationships remain excellent and communication is frequent, friendly and helpful on both sides. GEC went on to manage its second programme and ALP launched the first module of the UK rolling programme.

Re-entry of participants

One of our continuing concerns was to help participants understand something of the experience as a whole even as they entered the first stage. One particular example is the need for the participant to keep alive in his mind his relationship with his own nominating company, while working daily with another, and to come to terms with the situation he may face on his return. He should surely be consciously accepting his own development and the effects this may have on his relationships with those he has left behind, but will meet again. As all course designers know, this is a difficult problem. Project work and a high degree of relevance in course work all help to reduce the difficulty experienced in this re-entry phase. Nonetheless there are real problems, and we are developing ways of improving the opportunities for participants to work at these in future programmes.

And the future?

The GEC experience has already been used in a number of new activities — for example, the design of the Nehru project in India and of a rolling programme with a consortium of companies in the UK. This carries its own dangers. We are walking a tightrope where we try to maintain the newness and the attack of action learning — the green-field approach in any situation — while yet learning from experience. We are resisting the packaging of a programme, but we are building up knowledge of what constitutes a programme. We have continuously to re-examine with people in each new situation the criteria by which design decisions are made, yet we must not keep on reinventing the wheel. Just now when development work leaps on apace, we are in little danger. New situations present themselves, new ideas come easily. Variety of opportunity will keep our approach lively and creative. Will we be able to maintain this when action learning is more established and respectable? If *we* are no longer learning, we shall be blocking instead of releasing other people's potential.

Part Four
The impact of action learning on GEC

13
We'd do it again

Two GEC managers review the project carried out in their company

CLEM JANSEN and DON SINCLAIR

> Clem Jansen is managing director of GEC Electrical Projects Ltd and GEC Industrial Controls Ltd. Prior to taking up these two appointments in 1972, Mr Jansen was managing director of GEC-Elliott Process Automation Ltd and before that managing director, GEC-Elliott Traffic Automation Ltd, which is the company he joined in GEC in 1967.
>
> Don Sinclair is director, technical services, GEC Electrical Projects Ltd and GEC Industrial Controls Ltd, previously having held positions of chief engineer, general manager and works director in the latter company. Prior to this he held senior engineering positions in AEI heavy plant division.

Our company designs, manufactures and sells a wide range of standard, semi-standard and custom-built products. The need for the project arose because it was experiencing increasing difficulty in achieving the required improvement in performance. Return on capital employed, inventory, stocks and work in progress and overall productivity were giving cause for concern. This was happening in spite of a satisfactory order book and consistent management pressures.

The problems were further aggravated by the recent introduction of some newly developed products, a rapidly expanding market and the need for tighter performance targets. Also there were serious material supply problems and a general pressure on cash flow, coincidental with critical loading conditions in certain of the company's feeder departments.

The business had recently been divided into product groups, each serving specific market areas with its own allocated resources. Conditions were now ready for the introduction of business systems suited specifically to the needs of each of these product units. A further factor giving cause for concern was that we had been engaged for some time on a rigorous policy of component and product standardization. By now there should have been more tangible evidence that the measures were beginning to pay off.

The project was seen by us as an opportunity to study each function of one particular product group and devise more streamlined and simpler procedures to meet the specific needs of that unit. It would involve analysing the requirements of the information flow between the activities of marketing, design, procurement and manufacture. We hoped for the development of a model of the business which would enable the optimum operating parameters to be defined. The comparison between the actual results achieved and those planned would enable a measure of business efficiency to be derived. The data generated would give a more reliable basis for forward planning of the business concerned.

It was envisaged that the project would result in a significant reduction in the volume of paperwork by simplifying the procedures and by avoiding duplication of indirect effort. This would serve as a basis for computerization of the business systems at some time in the future. It was anticipated that the exercise could set the pattern for other product groups operating in the company and maximize the use of common systems. It was also expected that it would result in a streamlining of information flow for top management purposes and thereby increase the effectiveness of the overall company operations.

A stranger in the organization

A fresh mind certainly assists a company to reassess its own problems from new angles. The stranger participant asks questions that frequently do not occur to those engaged in the business. The questions give rise to answers which stimulate a new approach to the task in hand. An investigator who is not a member of the management team has time to talk and listen and has not 'heard it all before'.

The fact that the participant has the support of top management to investigate all aspects of the company, and has free access to any information required, stresses the need for him to establish good relationships with all those with whom he comes into contact. The success of his endeavours depends materially on the manner in which he uses these privileges. Once he has established himself as an ally and dispelled any suspicion that he has been planted as a spy, a great deal of benefit can accrue to the organization. All those involved are able to talk freely and express their views and ideas when they know that confidentiality will be respected.

This particular approach stimulated action at the working level and in fact released a fund of ideas not normally tapped during day-to-day working. The participant was successful in bringing out this dormant potential and in getting individuals who may not be organizationally related to work together as a team with one common aim in view. A most important element in the effectiveness of the participant is that he has time to listen to what is said, free from the day-to-day pressures of line responsibility. There is no doubt that any management can become immunized to its own problems by continual exposure to them.

Impact of the project on the business

There was little short-term impact resulting from the project, and no formal solution to the problem as originally set. This confirmed for us our original belief as to the main problem areas. Also, it gave us a clear indication that we have the potential in the company to solve our own problems if the approach, attitude and management are correct. The project demonstrated the value of setting to work on the problem an outsider who had access to external experts and regular meetings with colleagues in his project set. He was also able to devote the whole of his time to the task in hand.

Since the programme, the company has adopted in one or two different ways the basic principles involved in action learning. For example, one man has been seconded for three months from his normal duties. He has produced recommendations of importance to the business of one product group, and these are being implemented. This man worked alone without the value of a project set. Even without this added dimension the impact of his work was impressive. In another case, three senior men were brought together for a concentrated period to look into a vital business procedure influencing our export capability. Their recommendation has also produced action.

Tackling the problem as a formal project has value in that all parts of the organization involved are consulted, and the discussions which follow form a valuable forum for exchanging views and ideas. Whilst no dramatic innovation was achieved the exercise certainly contributed towards the introduction of procedures which had been discussed but up till then had been given a lower priority. This accelerated the tempo of the activity. But more importantly we saw changes taking place in our participant. His self-awareness increased and we now felt certain that his ability to cope with managerial situations was growing. On the strength of this, our recommendation after the programme was to give him a substantive managerial responsibility immediately, rather than wait.

The formal project approach confirmed beyond question the value of action learning, particularly in the information which could be derived from liaison with other industries dealing with similar problems and with projects encountering common objectives. Also the formal approach contributes materially to the effort and enthusiasm that can be brought to bear on the problem.

The value of the method

We would not hesitate to employ this technique again; in fact variations on the basic theme of action learning are already in operation, as mentioned above. Many useful lessons were learned which would do much to ensure that the most serious mistakes would not be repeated in future:

1 Certain fundamental issues need clarifying in the early stages between the client and the participant.
2 The project must be monitored regularly.
3 The participant should have a strong interest in the type of problem to be solved.
4 The client organization must define its problem clearly from the outset.
5 Before the project is started, adequate dialogue should take place between both parties to ensure that there is a common understanding, objective and interest.
6 Solid lines of communication should be established.
7 Regular communication between the client and the participant is vital.
8 The client should not allow the project to diverge from the set course, but the participant must be given freedom to approach the problem in the manner he/she sees fit.

14
You don't need to be an expert

GEC's group personnel manager reviews his experiences as a set adviser

GLYN TROLLOPE

>Four personnel specialists from GEC took part in the programme in the key roles of set advisers. All were senior men — three personnel directors of major divisions and the group personnel manager, Glyn Trollope. Mr. Trollope has written this chapter from his own point of view, but each of the others has had experiences on a similar scale.
>
>Glyn Trollope joined Osram (GEC) Ltd as personnel manager in 1963. Previously he worked in Richard Thomas & Baldwin Ltd and ICI. He is now group personnel manager for GEC as a whole.

In a chapter like this, one has to reveal too much of oneself for comfort. But that, I believe, is part of action learning. Reading philosophy at university had opened my eyes to the importance of objectivity and self-examination. Action learning offered a new opportunity to increase my understanding of myself and others at work.

First impressions

Initially, in spite of the special appeal of the word action within GEC, I was cynical about the programme. The team in which I usually work is exceptionally participative and I considered that we practised action learning every day of our working lives.

Looking back, however, I had missed the point that even good teamwork can be improved and some of my initial cynicism probably stemmed from uncertainty about my own competence to cope with a completely new situation. I had a reasonable track record — especially in industrial relations — but how would I fare in the novel role as an internal GEC project adviser? I now realize more clearly how uncertain most people are in the face of change and the unknown and that it is the quality of response which is all-important.

Along with an external project adviser I was involved with a set of four GEC managers and one Post Office manager with projects in microelectronics, turbine generators, gas appliances, electronic instrumentation and valves. A bewildering galaxy of topics for a project adviser who was neither scientist nor engineer. The combination of external and internal project advisers was an important feature of the process; without the external adviser the programme would have been over-influenced by GEC styles. I missed the opening two weeks of the programme at Dunchurch Industrial Staff College and I remember being very impressed with the team spirit that had developed amongst participants by the time we first met together. My introduction to the group was friendly. But I recall being irritated by the group brand of humour — until I realized that they had tensions to unwind — and I resented not sharing the jokes and not yet being part of the set. Perhaps the group should have been more aware of their effect on a newcomer.

These perceptions are part of the process of action learning. And the experiences are commonplace in work situations — but it is unlikely that I would have thought sufficiently along these lines had I not been involved in the programme. Whilst I am convinced that 'flair' is an essential and indefinable ingredient in getting the best out of people, it helps if one finds the time and the help of others to think clearly, constructively and objectively about how this can be achieved, especially since some managers have less flair than others. This time for thought contrasts with the lack of time most people find to think ahead when they are doing their normal jobs. Action learning gives participants reasonable opportunities to think and take stock through the eyes of others. Inevitably, some participants have limitations which cannot be remedied. And it is counterproductive to highlight characteristics which a participant cannot control or improve. But most individual talents and characteristics can be developed. So within our project set, in the process of seeking solutions to problems, we tried to improve our abilities to listen, analyse and learn, and to recognize and improve various personal inadequacies which impede effective management.

My role in the set

As a project adviser I tried to concentrate on the participants, their projects and learning experiences. We found it of paramount importance that discussions should be as uninhibited as possible. This could have been difficult for a number of reasons — especially because of my central GEC role as group personnel manager. But soon after meeting we talked about this in the context of assurances that had been given about the confidential nature of project set discussions. Largely due to the participants' response we then forgot that I was group personnel manager — unless it suited us to remember. And then I benefited very significantly by listening to my colleagues' views on a wide range of topics relevant to GEC.

A project adviser needs to gain respect without trying to dominate the set. I found this difficult at first. Fairly frequently in my job I have to make the running and lead discussions. I tried to play down this tendency, and I was helped by many of the projects being well above my head — at least at first. Naïve questions, however, helped to clarify issues and in the process I was learning as well. Some of the projects involved clarification of complex problems rather than clearcut solutions. Inevitably, the terms of reference of projects changed as a result of initial investigations. This should be avoided but in a few cases projects were so complicated or central to particular businesses that it was too much to expect one participant to achieve significant conclusions. This serves to emphasize the necessity of selecting and defining projects very carefully — so that it is feasible for participants to achieve solutions. Or, alternatively, perhaps, for several people to concentrate on one complex problem and solve it together as a team.

Two of the participants in our set were tackling projects within GEC businesses different from their own. One participant came to GEC from the Post Office and two others attempted projects related to their normal GEC jobs, each in a different way. One of our projects was neither solved nor, at times, handled very well and, for a period, tended to monopolize the set's discussions. Basically, the difficulty was caused through lack of commitment by a client company. At an early stage I wanted to raise the problem directly with the company concerned, in my capacity as group personnel manager. But the set felt this was inappropriate since my role as set adviser should be operated from within the set itself. Try as we might, we failed as a set to help the particular participant achieve his project aims. The danger of the situation I have described is that the participant tends to bear the brunt of the blame. This is unfair in circumstances where the company has a low commitment to the project problem in the first place.

The set at work

When we met as a set, the participants discussed their ideas and problems — sometimes on the basis of papers circulated previously. These meetings often took place at the units where projects were being undertaken. Occasionally, presentations involved too much narrative or there was lack of order and clarity both in presentation and response. However, as the programme progressed people improved the ways in which they marshalled their thoughts and presented material. The most productive discussions occurred on recognition of hitherto elusive problems. When this happened it was a question of discussing the most effective means of helping the participant to find solutions. This is what action learning tries to achieve.

Questioning, listening and learning were the key activities that we tried to practise in project set meetings — but not always successfully. Sometimes questions clouded rather than clarified meanings or the group did not respond adequately to the needs of a participant. Occasionally, participants could not or would not recognize problems, let alone face up to them. As a group we tried as best we could to identify these difficulties and respond to each others' needs in practical ways. The questioning approach was essentially supportive and this was especially important when participants lacked confidence.

The objectives were to help rather than to duel, attack or score points. And if participants wanted to 'rehearse' the trends of their investigations with their colleagues this was readily accepted by the set. Thinking aloud about problems helped participants to clear their minds and was in itself therapeutic. In the face of the tasks ahead individuals' self-doubts were reflected overtly, and sometimes obliquely, through behaviour within the set. In the early stages some of us expressed ourselves badly, or were more interested in expressing our points of view rather than listening to colleagues and learning from the experience. Others were determined to shock and reflected consciously or subsconsciously the need to draw attention to themselves. There were different sorts of cries for help — both intellectual and emotional — which we had to try to recognize and respond to as best we could.

At a very early stage, the anxieties and uncertainties of some clients about the programme were relayed, often unwittingly, by participants. In the whole programme only a few projects did not stand a chance of succeeding from the start — either for client or participant. I think that this was more of a reflection on the people than the programme.

Successful senior managers need to be selfstarters; able participants inevitably succeed despite the shortcomings of other participants, clients, project advisers or, for that matter, projects. Overcoming problems is what successful management is all about.

At times, project set discussions were too unstructured for my liking. This was because no one was really responsible for managing each session. It reminded me of some nonconformist prayer meetings where everyone waits for someone else to start! In this respect the programme was too easygoing and did not correlate with my day-to-day experience of managing when, without domineering or stifling the contributions of others, it is essential to have a clear management focal point in coping with difficult problems. The programme did not preclude this, of course, but the set did not decide that this approach was important. If, however, it had been understood from the outset that project set discussions must be managed by participants in rotation this would not have detracted from the value of the programme. Indeed the learning process could have been enhanced.

Link with the client

Participants would also have benefited from much closer links with their particular client, without inhibiting in any way the importance of self-discovery and improvement. It was as though some clients — especially those involved in 'own-job' projects — left far too much to the programme. The development of participants was not seen by them sufficiently as an integral part of their managing. Action learning is relevant beyond a six- or nine-month programme. It is a *way of managing* which, provided it does not become obsessional, can continue to produce positive results through people. Clients should manage action learning projects as effectively as they manage other aspects of their businesses.

Has action learning developed me?

I find it very difficult to assess the way in which the programme has helped in my development. In my career to date, development has resulted from response to new problems, responsibilities and situations. Frequently, these have occurred in crises and often there has been insufficient time to reflect on performance. But the learning curve has been steep. I had more time to reflect as a project adviser —

although it was only a part-time assignment. And when the disciplined objectivity of a programme is introduced, the learning curve can be even steeper.

There were several new experiences for me — including exposure to science-based projects. Initially, I had healthy doubts about my ability to cope. But I soon realized that everyone had a contribution to make and it became clear that a combination of different talents within a team can be invaluable. Although there were times when I wanted to take the programme 'by the scruff of the neck' the discipline of being subject to the decisions of the set was good for me. It helped to control an inbuilt impatience and a relatively strong drive for achievement; I learned to see new forms of achievement.

We seldom really take stock of the way in which we manage. My experience of action learning will always be a reminder of the need for periodic reflection. I am not saying that the results of these evaluations will necessarily be effective — although I hope that they will. But I will try all the harder because of the influence of this programme of action learning.

This programme in perspective

The initial action learning programme was not the beginning of significant developments or changes within GEC. The decision to run the programme was effect rather than cause since change was already under way. But this did not diminish the role of the programme in providing a platform for people to discuss a wide range of topics affecting the company. These included business performance ratios, research, development and investment as well as personnel policies including communications, consultation and involvement. These discussions were important to participant managers and the company. Participants met and talked with GEC's managing director and the managing directors of operating companies.

Many myths and apocryphal stories were put into perspective. But when participants were not satisfied with explanations they persisted in their criticisms and were not inhibited. These discussions, although sometimes bordering on complaint sessions, put the company more in touch with an important level of management and this was a significant byproduct of the programme. Similarly the programme developed and improved rather than created working relationships between central personnel department and our operating company colleagues.

During 13 years with the company I have seen developments which increasingly recognize the importance of people within GEC. The company's performance in this respect was discussed fearlessly and frequently within the programme. It was clearly advantageous that participants could talk freely with members of central personnel department and the personnel directors of several operating companies. And that we could listen and respond. This relationship was especially important towards the end of the programme.

In a decentralized company — where each business has to decide who is to be employed — there is risk involved in a participant leaving a job for nine months in search of experience which should lead to positive career development — not necessarily within his own business. In a business organized as GEC is, there could be no guarantee of the next job and in a few cases the subsequent offer of jobs did not materialize until the effect on the participant was unsettling and (to say the least) sometimes unnerving. Before offers of employment materialized in these difficult circumstances, it was a question of trying to keep morale as high as possible and then, in response to individual requests, being prepared to think aloud about alternative job prospects. And thus help a participant to decide on the next stage of career progression. But in the end, the responsibility rested on the man himself with help and support from the company.

I have tried to reflect some of the pros and cons of action learning from the point of view of an internal project adviser. Clearly some participants thought that the programme was a huge success, others thought the programme failed and others only saw through a glass darkly. What do I think?

Many management training courses involve a lot of work and pressure without being all that relevant to real-life situations. While they last, many of these 'assault courses' can make intellectual and emotional demands on people without meaning very much subsequently. Whilst I recognize the importance of formal training and education in the techniques of managing, the most significant growth in management ability comes through the help and example of good managers at work setting high and challenging standards. I am convinced that action learning programmes at many levels can be invaluable in this respect in developing a business and tackling its problems. The programmes need competent tutor/managers with participative style who will get the best out of a group of people who, from the outset, recognize that if the programme does little or nothing for them it is probably because they have done little or nothing for the programme.

15
It's opening our minds
What the process of action learning has started in GEC

MIKE BETT

> One view from the central personnel department in GEC's head office was given in the previous chapter. Mike Bett also works from Stanhope Gate. Since his contact with the day-to-day activities of the programme was minimal, he had a chance to observe the prime effects of the whole thing more objectively than most.
>
> Mike Bett is personnel director of GEC. Formerly he was director, industrial relations, at the Engineering Employers' Federation. He has an honours degree in history from Cambridge, and is a fellow of the Institute of Personnel Management.

To claim that action learning is now permeating management development throughout GEC operating companies would be an over-enthusiastic exaggeration, or at best premature. But it has taken root as an approach to the solution of management problems. And most of those who have participated in, or observed, the two programmes that have taken place, are persuaded of the value of tackling real problems as opposed to case studies. So far, the only formal application of the action learning approach has involved the middle stratum of managers across the company. The second programme has seen modifications of our original design so as to adapt it more to the needs of the operating companies. Future programmes will no doubt continue to evolve to meet those needs as they shift.

In fact, the problem of developing action learning programmes and getting them off the ground has been a project in itself. Those closely involved have learnt from the experience — not so much about management development programmes as about overcoming the difficulty of introducing something new to managers who have hitherto survived reasonably successfully without it.

Nevertheless, the most immediately recognizable benefit which the action learning programmes have brought has been an opening up of minds. The participants, the company project advisers and indeed the managers who have either been involved as clients or who have come to Dunchurch to talk about their businesses, have all benefited. In the past it has not been the practice in GEC, because of its decentralized structure, for managers from different units to meet and share their problems and experience. This has meant that full use has not been made of the expertise and ingenuity available — an uncharacteristic waste of resources.

Now, to a modest degree as yet, managers who have come into contact with the action learning programmes are beginning to appreciate the value, to each of them as individuals as well as to the company, of developing a less individualistic more cooperative team approach to management. It is significant that this comes at a time when the operating company managements are all concentrating more than ever on improving communication and consultation so as to achieve greater employee involvement and satisfaction.

Certainly the action learning programmes have proved a most successful way of revealing where communications from and to the top are not functioning properly. It has been most instructive to know what the young up-and-coming managers who have participated in the programmes believe are the directives from on high that determine the attitudes and policies of their immediate superiors. It has been disturbing to learn just how much middle management believes that its proposals, ideas and aspirations are blocked on the way up by senior managers, who apparently believe that in doing so they are responsibly interpreting and applying company policy determined at Stanhope Gate. Indeed, the need to persevere with improving communications between middle and senior management — not only through the normal hierarchical structure, but also by senior managers plugging in *ad hoc* at levels with which they do not normally come into contact — is probably the most important lesson those involved have learned.

As for the future, the value of a programme which involves participants from many different GEC companies has been proved. Such programmes will be repeated. But there are other settings in which action learning principles can be applied. Individual businesses can set up their own programmes for different levels of management and supervision; or they can combine managers from different levels and disciplines in exercises designed to produce management teams for the present and the future. All these ideas are being considered carefully.

Whatever way action learning may be adapted to the needs of GEC companies, the object will always be to encourage managers to examine the habits of mind they have acquired and to become more receptive to new solutions to familiar management problems. The ideal would be for unselfish teamwork, plus the modest willingness to question, listen and learn, to permeate all management behaviour and not just management development programmes. Action learning promotes all of these virtues.

16
Action learning and the company

A project adviser, who is also a professor of business policy, takes the broad view

PROFESSOR TONY ECCLES

> Tony Eccles, ex shopfloor fitter, ex factory production manager, is now Professor of Business Policy at Glasgow University. His role in GEC evolved during and after the action learning programme. Because he became personally involved, he was able to see the company in the round, from an outsider's point of view.

GEC was a surprise to me. Having worked on management development programmes with other big British companies I had expected the worst. One programme had been in a management where people constantly sniped at each other, jockeyed for advantage, with a high rate of staff turnover, and where managers in their thirties looked worn beyond repair. I had expected the bigger and more successful GEC to be a vicious, more brutalized version of the same — with managers not only able but eager to eat each other (and me) for breakfast. Furthermore, I had an outsider's view of GEC, namely that it was a one-man band playing only the tune of a powerful leader who was uninterested in anything but financial efficiency and ruthless in cutting out any operation which faltered even momentarily.

The realities of GEC were much more reassuring. First, there was the organizational sophistication. Far from being a one-man band, GEC was a group of over 100 autonomous businesses grouped into six sectors. Each business had to present its plans for the coming year to the central management and then it had to go off and carry them out. Help could be made available if things went wrong; failure would be accepted only if the problems lay outside the influence of the business and, even then, it was expected that the local management would succeed in generating alternative plans. The responsibility was clearly put on those who carried out the actions. Unit managers were put in the bind that, although they had to submit their plans and have them monitored by the central management, the headquarters did not take on the responsibility for the outcome. Plans were not 'approved'. The business was simply told that if that was what it wanted to do, then it should go ahead and do it — and be responsible for the results.

This system has diffused responsibility widely through the management of the company, and it is axiomatic that you take responsibility for the operation which you control. Although there can be grey areas — particularly on multi-product, multi-business sites — the system is usually clear and is the antithesis of the management structures where power is diffused through committees and groups so that, in the end, nobody is responsible for the results.

It is not surprising that the senior divisional and business managers in GEC are known as the 'barons'. This medieval analogy is apt. You may, as the manager of a GEC business, owe allegiance to the central group, but you 'own' your territory and are responsible for it. The result is that the centre cannot readily tell people what to do — it can only advise them. If they choose to ignore suggestions then they stand or fall by the consequences of their judgement. Some of the suggestions can be pretty powerful, but there is some genuine leeway and GEC is more of a federation than the centralized autocracy which is usually perceived from outside.

It all makes GEC a very political organization in that the power base, performance and ideas of an influential manager are major sources of his strength. More than that, GEC will cheerfully admit to being political. This is an appealing change from organizations where discussion of organizational politics is illregarded because they seek to pretend that unified and dispassionate logic forms the sole basis of their decisions. Such organizations may also be saying that flair and leadership are not highly regarded either, for once you define politics as the struggle to obtain and hold power in order to influence events, then can any manager be competent without being adroitly political? GEC looked very interesting.

The action learning programme reached the company when GEC was already in a transitional stage. The absorption of AEI and English Electric was almost complete but the experience had been painful.

ACTION LEARNING AND THE COMPANY

Cutting out duplications, even triplication, of facilities had cost thousands of jobs. GEC had shown it could prune, but could it grow?

Large sums were being spent on research and development, plus investment in products and the machinery to manufacture them. Turnover and profits were still rising. But how would the company move on to the next stage? Interest was growing in worker involvement, in better communications and in spreading the senior management's concern for efficiency more widely through the organization. The obvious place to start was in the middle management — rich in numbers, the source of future general managers, directly in control of shopfloor and technical processes, and possessing basic skills well worth developing to greater levels of effectiveness.

The businesses could continue to develop people by throwing them in at the deep end. But there are limits to the occasions where that is appropriate for, as Professor John Morris has pointed out, it tends to induce a state known as drowning. And what if the business drowns along with the floundering manager?

The opposite choice was not so enticing; it would have been against GEC's whole ethos to nurse people along so that they became institutionalized and would just carry out current practice with negligible innovation or risk. The withdrawal of the nurse might also reveal embarrassing vulnerabilities.

The action learning method fitted GEC's culture closely. It was based on intervention not detachment, it looked at real business problems in vivid business situations, the themes were current, not historical, and you had to stand by your views against those who would reap the results of your judgements. Both the first and second programmes were quite successful. People did develop their flair, their judgement, their skill, their confidence; problems were partly or extensively solved. The frank discussion of blemishes and dilemmas elsewhere in this book should not divert readers from these simple points. Nor should one ignore the growing support in and out of GEC for the third programme.

The concurrent developments in GEC do not make it easy to distinguish the effects of action learning separately though it is quite clear that it assisted and modified other developments in the company. However, it would be fair to make the following points:

1 It was possible to combine personal development with improvements in organizational effectiveness.
2 People could tackle projects closely associated with their own jobs and not be sucked back into their normal routines.

3 The participant's project work (and his absence) did help to develop his subordinates so that two groups of people were developed.
4 The third group to be influenced were the clients — not all favourably — who exposed their organizations to discreet but intelligent external surveillance (external because even if the participant was a local manager, his project set certainly was not).
5 Participants were given a licence to take on a general management role — though the licence was sometimes provisional. Most used it with the discretion of maturity, a few seemed to baulk at the riskiness and visibility of the role and remained technical analysts of the problems as specified for them.
6 One or two participants, their vision and opportunity widened, found it difficult to resist the temptation to embark on an evangelical mission to save the organization from itself.
7 Equally, the client managers could feel wary at the possibility that the project would go out of control — their control that is. Hints of this worry are implicit in Chapter 13, culminating in the claims that the client should define the problem and that 'The client should not allow the project to diverge from the set course ...' These are not claims which all participants and clients would support.

There are four direct statements which can be made to show the programme's effects on GEC:

1 Senior GEC managers have shown extensive willingness to visit the programmes — not just to instruct the participants, and not just to explain what they are doing — but to debate why they act as they do and to discuss choices of future strategy.
2 The participants show increased ability and willingness to consider wider corporate issues as they go through the programme and a healthier, less accepting spirit of inquiry has marked their individual confidence and skill.
3 The programme has further amplified consideration of more open and more knowing choices of style of control, of management, and the development and encouragement of talents.
4 Finally, there is the development which was summed up in the late President Eisenhower's alleged injunction to his hyper-interventionist Secretary of State, John Foster Dulles: 'Don't just do something. Stand there!'

Defining the project problem has become recognized as a major and underrated part of the project work itself. The value of the participant tackling it is in the novelty which he can bring to the project analysis. Were the problem easily defined by the incumbent managers, then resources could have been diverted to its solution. Indeed, in GEC, had the problem been accurately defined it would probably have been bludgeoned to death.

But problems are slippery, and their persistence is a measure of their intractability. 'We have a problem of inventory control' can easily unfold as 'Our inventory control difficulty is a symptom of a problem in our wage payment scheme but the implications are so gruesome that we prefer not to consider them'. This is not to claim that every stated obstacle has a differing underlying reality — only that a willingness to let the participant follow his intelligent nose may pay off more than having to jump through the client's already constructed hoops. It is a measure of GEC's continuing development that more tricky projects are being proposed by clients who are, in effect, now saying 'We have this symptom, we believe this to be the cause, please help us to find what the problem is and suggest how we might best solve it'.

Postscript
GEC's second and third programmes

The second programme in GEC has happened and the third began in October 1976. The second had fourteen participants, in three sets. Eleven were from GEC, one from ICI, one from the Ministry of Defence and one was a research officer with the EETPU (formerly the ETU). As ALP had made a policy decision not to take part in the second programme, the term 'external adviser' was coined for the role previously played by ALP advisers. Two men introduced to GEC by ALP — Tony Eccles and Bob Garratt — stayed on for the second programme. Geoff Gaines joined DISC to become the third external adviser and to look after the DISC end of coordination and administration. David Pearce remained as overall programme coordinator, and once again there was a GEC adviser to each set, two being the top personnel executives from large GEC operating companies and the third the director of the Marconi Staff Development Centre.

The first programme had obviously set off numerous shock waves — it was important to maintain the momentum by launching a second programme quickly. On the second programme there was a higher proportion of own-job or own-site projects. This presented a challenge. There was one genuine exchange project and one joint (two-man) project. The rest were own-site and about half were own-job. The programme was launched just as soon as 14 participants had been mustered.

The duration of the second programme was six months compared with eight in the first programme. The second three months, following the Christmas break, seemed frighteningly short, with the implementation phase still a long way off in many people's minds. On the other hand, there is little doubt, with hindsight, that the problems lay less in the absolute time available than in the participants' perceptions about time (too time-sensitive too early). The organizers, too, were insufficiently aware of the need for tighter planning on a shorter programme. However, the own-jobbers found that implementation happened as a matter of course — and could be completed after the programme ended, if need be.

The second time round was easier in some ways than the pioneering adventure of the first — the experience was not brand new and the number of people involved was smaller. Participants' expectations were rather better defined and, perhaps, more realistic; many more were working in environments — even jobs — with which they were familiar. Predictably, the second programme was less dramatic, less noisy than its predecessor.

Everyone is now in a job, some promoted, some completing implementation, some in a stretched version of their old role. The feedback was highly favourable, with one or two exceptions. The set was considered to be a powerful learning vehicle; clients and nominators were aware that participants had visibly grown, were more aware of the situations in their companies and more capable of handling them; progress had been made in the projects. Some of the 'mistakes' of the first programme were put right in the second. Most — to judge from the similarity of feedback from participants in each programme — were repeated. Gaining client commitment; handling the eventual re-entry trauma; coordinating and planning the formal, residential phases; involving the client during the course of the programme; evaluating the programme; sets communicating better with each other: all these could have been done better.

Some specific points have been raised regularly at the various review meetings called to consider the first and second Developing Senior Managers Programmes (DSMP). Here are some of them:

1 The total success of the activity may be severely marred by insufficient discussion and preparation in the participant's nominating company. This problem is often not observed until much later when the question of re-entry crops up — perhaps at a time when project implementation is at its most sensitive. Though it may be impossible to predict what individuals and organizations will look like in six months' time, it is essential that a firm basis for continuing and frank dialogue exists between all involved. Programme organizers will be happy to advise.
2 The 'perfect model' of an action learning programme does not

exist. The programme is, therefore, open to constant question and review. Participants, clients and nominators should be encouraged, or feel free, to challenge and demand much more than they have tended to in the past, whilst the programme is going on.

3 The client is much more of a key figure than he normally perceives himself to be. His commitment to the project solution, his personal involvement in the programme, his willingness to re-examine and where necessary redefine the project in the light of experience and investigation, his very availability to the delegate and the programme, are all prerequisites for real success.

4 There is an inevitable, and in many ways essential, 'floundering' period at the beginning, when it may seem — to all concerned — that time is being wasted and little achieved. This is partly technical — being connected with sorting out the red herrings before arriving at the final and true project definition — and partly the result of a very valuable experience the delegate is going through. Probably for the first time in his working life he is being required to be self-motivated, self-directed, self-paced, and the adjustment is often confusing and uncomfortable.

5 DSMPs are not — or not exclusively — for crown princes. Part of the value of the experience comes from the blend of participants with every kind of baton in their knapsack, from captain to field-marshal.

6 Outsiders (be they participants, project advisers, lecturers or guest speakers) are of particular value for the extra and wider perspective they bring.

7 DSMP kills many myths — particularly about GEC and the way it is run. Sometimes it confirms them also, but this time on the basis of evidence and experience.

8 Really significant business problems can rarely be 'solved' in six months, and in many cases there is no complete solution. The way to approach solutions can, however, often be identified in this period.

Geoff Gaines is coordinator of the third programme with David Pearce acting in an advisory capacity. The main concern will be not to change the basic model too much, but rather to work hard on getting right those mistakes carried over from the first to the second programme. However, there is one very important change. In the first programme a mix of 'exchange' and 'own-job' projects occurred naturally. In the second, half were 'own-job' and most were 'own-site'. This indicated a swing towards the 'we can't afford to send a man away for six months' syndrome. When it comes to the third programme the offer document (see Appendix I for first programme offer document) contains this section on options available:

> OPTIONS
> A number of options are offered below and other suggestions could be considered provided they fit within the basic framework outlined. In order to ensure a balanced programme a reasonable distribution over the various options will be necessary. The preferred approach is for participants to broaden their experience by tackling a project in a different environment from the one they work in normally.
>
> (1) *Exchange between GEC operating companies*
> A participant will be nominated by one GEC operating company and allocated to a project in another completely separate operating company within GEC.
> (2) *Exchange within own GEC operating company*
> The participant will undertake a project in his own operating company or group of companies.
> (3) *Exchange with a non-GEC organization*
> This option involves a participant being nominated from a GEC operating company to undertake a project connected with an organization outside GEC, or vice versa. There can be two types of organization with which the exchanges can be arranged:
> *Either* An organization with some common interests, e.g. CEGB, Post Office, Ministry of Defence.
> *Or* Another company, whether in the engineering industry or not.

Notwithstanding these preferred approaches, it has proved to be interesting and valuable, in isolated cases, for participants to tackle some important feature(s) of their own job as a project. Thus, where a manager seems right for the programme, but cannot apparently be spared from his own job on a fulltime basis, it may well be worth discussing the idea of an 'own-job' project with the programme organizers.

In spite of this deliberate angling of the offer document for the third programme towards 'exchange' rather than 'own job', in the event the balance has remained about the same as it was in the second programme — i.e. half and half.

The third programme started in October 1976 and will run for six and a half months. After an initial three-week residential session, formal inputs will be short (one- to two-day) and regular (probably monthly) and will concentrate largely, but not exclusively, on the financial side of business. A 'representative system' will be strongly recommended to the sets and regular project adviser/representative meetings are planned.

Several new outside concerns are sending participants. It may even be that a fourth programme will have to be started while the third is still ongoing. GEC may reach sooner than expected that 'critical mass' of people (at least in many operating companies) who have been touched and convinced by action learning, so that spontaneous programmes can begin in-company. This should ensure the continuation of the activity where it belongs — in the company, self-generated and self-sustained.

But that is in the future. For now, GEC is concentrating on ensuring that the third programme does indeed succeed and that success and a standardized model do not go to its head. If action learning is ever viewed as not open to debate, it will be in danger of falling into complacency and that atrophy which has been the fate of too many robust management tools in the past.

Appendices

Appendix I
The offer document

The actual offer document issued within GEC is reproduced below

THE GENERAL ELECTRIC COMPANY LTD

DEVELOPING SENIOR MANAGERS

Contents

1 Objectives.
2 Participants.
3 The programme.
4 Options.
5 Projects.
6 Timing.
7 Charges.

March 1974

1 OBJECTIVES

The programme is designed to help able managers or specialists to learn, more usefully, quickly and comprehensively than might otherwise be the case, the skills required for more senior management jobs.

It also provides a means for important projects concerned with the improvement of the business to be undertaken.

2 PARTICIPANTS

The participant should have proved his worth in a management or specialist job.

He should have the necessary potential for promotion, following completion of his programme, to senior general management — or to a specialist job leading to senior general management — within five years.

The participant must be convinced that the programme will assist significantly in his development as a manager.

The majority of participants are likely to be in their 30s, but age is less important than an individual's capacity to develop his management ability for the mutual advantage of himself and the company.

3 THE PROGRAMME
The essence of the programme is that managers learn best by:

(a) Working on problems which are important to the success of the business.
(b) Reviewing their progress and problems in small groups with fellow participants on a regular basis.
(c) Being stimulated and helped by an experienced project adviser. The programme will provide one adviser to every four or five participants and they will meet every week or so.

4 OPTIONS
Within the basic framework outlined in section 3, above, a number of options are available. In order that the programme does not become unbalanced it will be necessary to ensure that there is a reasonable distribution over the various options. The preferred approach is for participants to broaden their experience by tackling a project in a different environment from the one they work in normally.

(1) *Exchange between GEC operating companies*
A participant will be nominated by one GEC operating company and allocated to a project in another completely separate operating company within GEC.
(2) *Remain in own GEC operating company*
The participant will undertake a project in a different part of his own operating company or group of companies.
(3) *Remain in own job*
This option is particularly suited to a participant who is about to be, or has recently been, promoted. He would participate in all the basic elements of the programme, namely the formal tuition sessions, regular meetings with fellow participants and receive the assistance of a project adviser. His new job would constitute the project.

APPENDIX I

(4) *Exchange with a non-GEC organization*
In this option, a participant would be nominated from a GEC operating company to undertake a project connected with an organization outside GEC. There are two types of organization with which the exchanges can be arranged:

Either   An organization with some common interests, e.g. CEGB, Post Office, Ministry of Defence.
Or   Another company, whether in the engineering industry or not.

An operating company wishing to take advantage of this option will need to identify and approach a suitable organization with which an exchange could take place. Every assistance will be given to arrange the necessary contacts. If the proposed project is also of interest to the other organization, a participant from each organization could be nominated to work on it jointly.

5 PROJECTS

The project should be concerned with a major business problem involving a broad understanding of the company. It should not be directed at the solution of problems which are exclusively technical.

The project should cover more than one function of the business requiring the involvement, cooperation and commitment of a number of other managers.

The participant will spend approximately six to nine months working on the project. After initial agreement on his task, he will diagnose the problems, make recommendations and then help to initiate the necessary action. It is desirable but not necessary for the project to be capable of being completed within the time allowed.

6 TIMING

May 1974	Nomination of participants and selection of projects.
June/July	Matching of participants to projects, and allocation of project advisers.
August/September	Occasional meetings between participant and project adviser, and with managing director of receiving company, to make the necessary preparations for starting the programme. These preparations will include reading and

	identification of necessary management techniques.
October	Fulltime participation begins with formal tuition at DISC provided by a selection of DISC tutors and high-calibre outside teachers.
November/December/ January	Diagnosis and investigation of the problem; weekly group meetings with fellow participants and project advisers.
February 1975	Period of consolidation at DISC; opportunities for participants to test their proposed recommendations on appropriate senior managers and external contacts.
March/April/May	Securing acceptance of recommended solutions and initiating implementation. Regular group meetings with fellow participants and project advisers.

7 CHARGES

The nominating company will, in addition to salary, pay the tuition costs. These will amount to approximately £2 500 per head, depending on the total number of participants.

The hotel, travelling, secretarial and other support costs incurred by the participant will be borne by the receiving company. In allocating participants to projects the desirability of minimizing the inconvenience to the individual and the expense to the receiving company will be taken into account.

Appendix II
Debate between set advisers and GEC staff

These are the raw, unedited notes taken immediately after a meeting held one evening at the halfway point in the programme. They are an honest record, and include all points of confusion and disagreement as well as consensus views. The discussion itself was unstructured – issues have been listed under headings for convenience.

Those present

Four GEC project set advisers.
Four ALP project set advisers.
Staff of Dunchurch Industrial Staff College (DISC).
GEC programme coordinator.
ALP programme coordinator.

What is management development?

1   It is about the development of the participants for the benefit of the organization.
2   It is about the development of the participants for the benefit of the participants.
3   It is an aspect of organizational development and has to be dealt with simultaneously for any real benefit for either party.
4   It is essentially disruptive and dangerous and needs to be very carefully controlled.
5   It is disruptive in the short-term but highly beneficial to the participants and total organization in the medium- and long-term as it introduces criticism, variety, and change within the organization.

The programme

1. Question whether it is being driven fast enough.
2. Question whether people who are firing on all four cylinders learn the most.
3. GEC culture stretches people by using other people who know what questions to ask.
4. If the programme is too far from GEC culture it loses credibility, if too close it isn't different.
5. Participants have recognized that they are more able to ask the question of how things are done around here, and see the dilemmas of senior management.
6. Question whether we need two types of programme in the future — one for exchanges and one for own-job options.
7. We must not lose the own-job option.
8. Need for a concerted view on the programme.

Objectives of project

1. Develop awareness of senior management responsibilities.
2. Develop awareness of senior management skills.
3. Solve a specific and complex GEC organizational problem.
4. Understand oneself.
5. Develop a sensitivity to the effect of oneself on others and vice versa.
6. Develop the ability to assess and take risks.
7. Develop the ability to take appropriate action.

Roles of the project adviser

ALP adviser

1. External critical approach.
2. Non-GEC set of experiences.

GEC adviser

1. Adviser on how to operate the present organizational structure.
2. Adviser on how to operate the financial and other policy rules.
3. Information-giver for relevant information within the organization.

Both advisers

1 Personal development tutor/friend.
2 Negotiator both within and outside the organization to facilitate the progress of the project.
3 Technical adviser, either personally or by pointing out others who know.
4 Process consultant.
5 Learning catalyst.
6 Problem-solving adviser.
7 Political adviser.

Selection of participants

1 Need to concentrate on the 'selfstarter'.
2 Need to concentrate on the non-selfstarters — i.e. the ones who 'seem to learn most from the projects'.
3 Need for careful screening of MDs and potential projects to ensure that they are relevant.
4 No need to ensure either of the above as this is part of the negotiation process which the participant will learn.
5 Need to ensure that the programme can counsel the company as well as the participant.
6 The quality of current participants is far too low and needs to be much higher in future.
7 There is no problem about the quality of the participants.

Selection of companies

1 Need for sufficient technical and organizational complexity to 'stretch' the participant.
2 The problem selected must be of immediate concern to the company, i.e. that they are interested in a fast and appropriate solution.
3 The senior management of the company show signs of needing management development themselves.
4 There should be no 'own-job *plus* project' option, i.e. there should be only two types of project:
   (a) Fulltime project in another organization.
   (b) Fulltime own-job as a project.

5 The companies be forced if using *(b)* above to look at their own management succession so that time is released for participant to participate truly in the project.

Style of project sets

1 Sets must be primarily task orientated.
2 Sets must be primarily process orientated.
3 Sets must be primarily problem-solving orientated.
4 Sets have to be a mixture of all three above, dependent on the characteristics of PA and participants.
5 Sets must move at a very fast pace.
6 Sets should move slowly at first building up to a fast pace.
7 Sets will move at various paces depending on circumstances which are not easily controllable.
8 We should install some sort of evaluation system so that at the end of the programme it would be possible to look at the effects of the different styles employed.

Learning and teaching

1 The most important element of the project is the 'teaching' that is done, i.e. the transmitting of information to participants.
2 The most important element of the project is the 'learning' that happens to the participants, i.e. those things that the participants select and take into themselves from amongst that which is transmitted.
3 The acquisition of knowledge is the critical element of the programme.
4 Knowledge is not the critical element for managerial tasks but the development of the relevant attitude and skills is.
5 A structured, i.e. more lecture-based, programme would ensure better learning.
6 'Structure' gives no correlation with what, when, where and how participants learn — people only learn when there is a *need* for them to learn.

Appendix III
List of participants and their projects

First GEC 'developing senior managers' programme (DSMP 1)

South-east project set

ALP project adviser   David Casey
GEC project adviser   Glyn Trollope
                                   (group personnel manager)

Participants in south-east project set

Name and age	David Carr (35)
Job	Divisional manager, power grid
Nominating company	English Electric Valve Ltd
Outline of project	Own-job
Client company	English Electric Valve Ltd

Name and age	Jim Cowie (38)
Job	Branch manager, technical and training
Nominating company	Post Office — Data processing services
Outline of project	Project management in GEC Turbine Generators Ltd
Client company	GEC Turbine Generators Ltd

Name and age	Colin Gaskell (37)
Job	Chief of new developments and processing
Nominating company	Marconi Instruments Ltd

Outline of project	Product policy and company growth.
Client company	Marconi Instruments Ltd
Name and age	John Newman (40)
Job	General manager, grocery division
Nominating company	Osram (GEC) Ltd
Outline of project	Reappraisal of range of cookers for home and export market.
Client company	Cannon Industries Ltd
Name and age	Bill Prince (40)
Job	Works director
Nominating company	GEC Walsall Ltd
Outline of project	To determine the optimum product policy for GEC Semiconductors Ltd.
Client company	GEC Semiconductors Ltd

North-west project set

ALP project adviser	Tony Eccles
GEC project adviser	Nigel Eldred (personnel director, GEC Power Engineering Ltd)

Participants in north-west project set

Name and age	Roger Benbow (37)
Job	General services manager
Nominating company	Ruston Paxman Diesels Ltd
Outline of project	Identifying and overcoming problems brought about by the extension of the product range with a new larger engine of unproven design.
Client company	Kelvin Marine Diesels
Name and age	Ron Biggs (33)
Job	Unit manager
Nominating company	GEC Telecommunications Ltd
Outline of project	Increase effective machine-shop output.
Client company	GEC Telecommunications Ltd

APPENDIX III

Name and age	Peter Henderson (30)
Job	Financial manager
Nominating company	AEI Cables Ltd
Outline of project	Initiate and implement job evaluation for divisional staff.
Client company	AEI Cables Ltd

Name and age	Graham Pound (37)
Job	Manufacturing control manager
Nominating company	Marconi Space and Defence Systems
Outline of project	GEC purchasing policy with particular reference to electrical components.
Client company	GEC Electrical Components Ltd

Name and age	Ian Smith (41)
Job	Contracts manager
Nominating company	GEC Industrial Controls Ltd
Outline of project	Own-job. To update/introduce necessary routines to ensure effective contract execution in a two-factory company with a revised organization based on product orientation.
Client company	GEC Industrial Controls Ltd

Name and age	John Wilesmith (29)
Job	Management services manager
Nominating company	GEC Telecommunications Ltd
Outline of project	Inventory control: setting up of inventory policies.
Client company	GEC Telecommunications Ltd

DISC south-east project set

ALP project adviser	Bob Garratt
GEC project adviser	John Shrigley (personnel director, GEC Electrical Components Ltd)

Participants in DISC/south-east project set

Name and age	Bryan Cooper (45)

APPENDIX III

Job	Manager, quality assurance
Nominating company	GEC Telecommunications Ltd
Outline of project	Changes to PO standards and specifications to improve exportability of transmission equipment.
Client company	GEC Telecommunications Ltd

Name and age	Don Howell (31)
Job	Company blade manager
Nominating company	GEC Turbine Generators Ltd
Outline of project	To help a major government department improve planning procedures by a study of current practices in the private sector.
Client company	Government department

Name and age	Barry Scott (32)
Job	Technical manager, mobile radio division
Nominating company	Marconi Communication Systems
Outline of project	To evolve discipline around product standardization.
Client company	GEC Industrial Controls Ltd

Name and age	Robin Smith (31)
Job	Head of group — transmission equipment development
Nominating company	Post Office
Outline of project	Changes to PO standards and specifications to improve exportability of transmission equipment.
Client company	GEC Telecommunications Ltd

DISC/Midlands project set

ALP project adviser	Jean Lawrence
GEC project adviser	James Pease-Watkin (personnel director, GEC Marconi Ltd)

Participants in DISC/Midlands project set

Name and age	John Chard (37)

Job	Contracts manager
Nominating company	GEC Electrical Projects, Rugby
Outline of project	Own-job
Client company	GEC Electrical Projects, Rugby

Name and age	Maurice Gates (52)
Job	Deputy manager — Lincoln
Nominating company	English Electric Valve Ltd
Outline of project	To manage Lincoln site.
Client company	English Electric Valve Ltd

Name and age	Keith Hodgkinson (30)
Job	Financial accountant
Nominating company	GEC Measurements Ltd
Outline of project	Study of distribution system to satisfy the needs of the business more economically.
Client company	Osram (GEC) Ltd

Name and age	Peter Howard (36)
Job	Manager, printed circuits
Nominating company	GEC Telecommunications Ltd
Outline of project	To identify changes in procedures and standards. To reduce the cost of production of printed circuit boards. (Joint project with Peter Preston from the Post Office).
Client company	GEC Telecommunications Ltd

Name and age	Peter Preston (36)
Job	Experimental officer and executive engineer
Nominating company	Post Office
Outline of project	To identify standards and acceptance procedures needed to minimize the cost of printed circuit boards. (Joint project with Peter Howard, GEC Telecommunications Ltd.)
Client company	GEC Telecommunications Ltd

Name and age	Peter Taylor (33)
Job	Product planning manager

Nominating company	GEC Telecommunications Ltd
Outline of project	Identify the best method of adapting PABXs to provide for data communication.
Client company	GEC Telecommunications Ltd

Glossary

ALP: Action Learning Projects International Ltd. A non-profit organization spreading action learning ideas in the UK and overseas. 97 Roe Lane, Southport, Merseyside PR9 7PD, England.
ALP PROJECT ADVISER: Project adviser provided by ALP.
BARON: See OPERATING COMPANY.
CLIENT: The person in the client organization who owns the problem and who therefore works closely with the participant on the project.
CLIENT ORGANIZATION: The organization which receives a participant to tackle its problem, expressed in the project.
DISC: Dunchurch Industrial Staff College, near Rugby.
DSMP: 'Developing Senior Managers' programme. The title used for each action learning programme at GEC.
GEC PROJECT ADVISER: A personnel director in GEC, acting as a project adviser and preparing to take the programme idea into GEC.
MANAGING BODY: See STEERING COMMITTEE.
MD: A managing director. Often the ultimate client and/or nominator, for a participant.
NOMINATOR: The person in the nominating company responsible for putting forward the participant for the action learning programme.
NOMINATING COMPANY: The company in which the nominator works — see NOMINATOR.
OPERATING COMPANY: A main business sector of GEC, often a cluster of companies, headed by an operating company managing director ('baron').
OWN-JOB PROJECT: A project in which a participant stays in his own job and tackles all of his job, or part of it, as a project.
PARTICIPANT: An individual undertaking a project on an action learning programme. From GEC operating companies, the Civil Service and the Post Office.

PROCESS: The means by which it is possible to distinguish between an objective and the method of reaching it.

PROJECT: The expression of the business problem, which is the vehicle by which the participant is able to help the organization reorganize its experiences, while the participant reorganizes his own.

PROJECT ADVISER: A catalyst used to develop social skills, problem-solving skills, and learning abilities in participants. They become progressively redundant as the project set takes responsibility for its own learning.

PROJECT SET: A group of four to six participants helping each other to learn via group criticism, aided by project advisers.

SPONSOR: See NOMINATOR.

STANHOPE GATE: The headquarters of the General Electric Company Ltd (1 Stanhope Gate, London W1A 1EH).

STEERING COMMITTEE: The group of GEC headquarters and operating managers who worked closely with ALP to develop and monitor the entire programme.

WORKSHOP: Designed and run by the participants, in which common problems or themes were investigated. Normally two days.